Unlocking the Scriptures for You

ROMANS

Bruce Shields

**STANDARD
BIBLE STUDIES**

STANDARD PUBLISHING

Cincinnati, Ohio   11-40106

Library of Congress Cataloging-in-Publication Data:

Shields, Bruce.
    Romans / by Bruce Shields
        p. cm. — (Standard Bible studies)
    ISBN 0-87403-166-4
    1. Bible. N.T. Romans—Commentaries. I. Title. II. Series.
BS2665.3.S55 1988
227'.107—dc19   88-2120
                                                                                    CIP

Copyright © 1988. The STANDARD PUBLISHING Company, Cincinnati, Ohio. A division of STANDEX INTERNATIONAL Corporation. Printed in U.S.A.

CONTENTS

PREFACE

It seems almost silly to write another commentary on Romans. There are hundreds available—many of them excellent works by outstanding scholars. Yet anybody who becomes deeply immersed in the book recognizes that it demands that we reread it regularly and deal with its deep thought, its strange power, yes, its divine revelation.

So I write, hoping that you will read and be motivated to read again Paul's epistle and to let its message rewrite the script of your life. This commentary is not technical in any sense. For the technicalities of language, history, and theology, you should turn to the two-volume International Critical Commentary by C. E. B. Cranfield or the volume by Ernst Kasemann. This book attempts to analyze relatively large portions of the text to see how Paul and the original recipients of the letter viewed the life of the Christian in its context in the Roman Empire of the first century. If we can catch that vision, we should be able to evaluate our own living as Christians in our culture and age.

If this commentary can accomplish that, it will also be helpful to those who teach and preach on texts from Romans, as I do. We all need help; so I write this with the prayer that it may be helpful.

Each chapter after the introduction begins with notes on the language of the text and on such historical, cultural, or doctrinal issues as are important to our understanding the meaning and impact of the text for its author and original recipients. The chapter concludes with a devotional/doctrinal message for the reader of Romans today.

The tension that has produced whatever creativity is present in this volume is caused by the conflict between the awareness of the dangers of oversimplification and the awareness of the futility of getting so technical that few, if any, people would actually read the book. So my purpose will be fulfilled if you read and gain help in understanding and in living from this slice of early Christianity. In fact, in order to profit from reading this commentary, it will be necessary for you to read the text of Romans alongside it. I further suggest that, along with the introduction, you read the whole epistle straight through, since that is how the apostle originally intended that it be heard.

An author is always conscious of his great debt to individuals and groups who have helped with the production of a work. I gladly acknowledge the European Evangelistic Society, under whose auspices and with whose encouragement I was able to do much of my research on Romans while I was ministering to the *Christliche Germeinde* (Christian Congregation) in Tuebingen, West Germany. I also offer my deep gratitude to my teacher, Peter Stuhlmacher of the University of Tuebingen, and to the many students at Lincoln Christian Seminary and Emmanuel School of Religion who helped me sharpen my understanding.

INTRODUCTION

The Author

In contrast to many of the other books of the New Testament, there is today no significant disputing of the claim that the apostle Paul is the author of the epistle to the Romans. The only question in this regard comes from the epistle itself and concerns the function of Tertius, who in Romans 16:22 identifies himself as the writer. This probably means that he was acting as Paul's stenographer, although he might have had some freedom of composition in some instances.

Paul, who until some time after his Damascus-road experience was known as Saul of Tarsus, was peculiarly well prepared to write this epistle. His home city, Tarsus, afforded what was perhaps the best training available for one who was to travel the Roman Empire with a message. It was situated not far from the Mediterranean Sea at an important juncture of both sea and land commerce. Thus, travel would have been both acceptable and accessible. Tarsus was also the capital of the Roman province of Cilicia, which at that time included Syria. Thus, Saul would have been familiar with the imperial government, especially as it operated in the provinces. Tarsus was also an outstanding center of Hellenistic education. Thus, Saul would have been exposed to the major philosophies of his day. One could hardly imagine better preparation for communicating to people around the empire than growing up in Tarsus.

But to understand the message he was to communicate and to deal with the natives of Palestine who were the first believers and communicators of the message, it was important that the preacher be a Jew. Saul was a namesake of the great hero of his tribe of Benjamin, the first king of Israel. He was, by his own report (Philippians 3:5, 6) reared in the strictest possible Jewish tradition—that of the Pharisees. It appears from Acts 21:37-40 that he spoke Greek and Aramaic equally well, which indicates that his family preserved the language of Israel by speaking it at home. So Saul/Paul knew firsthand the influence of the synagogues in Jewish communities around the empire and how those synagogues dispersed Jewish thought.

Finally, Paul's education prepared him for the specific struggle that arose around his missionary preaching. He had studied the *Torah*—the Jewish law—under Gamaliel, the outstanding rabbi of his day. Thus, he knew the way the Old Testament was used in undergirding arguments, as well as how the rabbis, most of whom were Pharisees and who were the leading authorities among first-century Jews, dealt with the law and life.

Saul first bursts onto the pages of Christian history in Acts 7 and 8, where we see him as a zealous firebrand—an educated Pharisee leading a Jewish persecution of Christians. On the threshold of a promising career, just when Saul felt himself following through on the legalistic logic of Pharisaism, the Lord revealed himself to him (Acts 9). Convinced that he was doing the will of God by demolishing faith in Jesus, who claimed to be the Messiah, Saul discovered that he was really persecuting the Messiah, the Son of God. But in spite of this mistake, God had a commission for Saul.

As one would expect, it took Saul time—several years, in fact (see Galatians 1:18 and 2:1)—to rethink things. He did not have to change his loyalty to God. His first priority was still to serve the God of his fathers. But he had to come to terms with Jesus Christ and His crucifixion and resurrection with reference to his background as a Pharisee. Once that was done and he was sent from Antioch to evangelize the rest of the empire, the man now called Paul became the leading spokesman of the faith.

The Date

The writing of Romans can with some confidence be dated around A.D. 56 or 57. Some scholars date it as early as 54, but that seems to me to be too early. There are two checkpoints of history that are used to fit Paul's missionary activities into a chronology: the term of Gallio as Proconsul of Achaia in 52 (see Acts 18:12) and Festus's succeeding Felix as Procurator of Judea in 60 (see Acts 24:27). Since Paul's stay in Corinth on his second missionary journey coincided with Gallio's arrival there, and since Festus came to Caesarea while Paul was in prison there, the writing of

Romans must fall between those dates. In fact, the information Paul gave in Romans about what he had accomplished and what he planned to do next (Romans 15:23-29) indicates that he was writing at the end of his third missionary journey, while awaiting the end of winter with his friends in Corinth. This is most likely the three-month period referred to in Acts 20:2, 3.

So Romans is one of the later epistles written by Paul, who had already made his three missionary journeys. He had been a Christian for over twenty years and a traveling evangelist for ten. He had written probably five of his New Testament epistles by this time. He was, in short, at the height of his creativity, having spent two decades working out his thinking about creation, redemption, revelation, and living in the light of Jesus the Messiah, and having seen his ideas proved in the laboratory of evangelism and church life all across the northeastern Mediterranean basin.

The Destination

It is not difficult to get general information about Rome in the first century, since it was the most important city in the world. Its population then was probably around 2,000,000. As capital of a mighty empire, the city was dotted with fine monuments and buildings used for governmental, cultural, and religious purposes.

The population itself was about half slaves. There were a few senators, knights, generals, priests, and their ilk, and the rest were bureaucrats, tradespeople, teachers, and laborers.

The founding of the Christian church in Rome is still shrouded in mystery. There is no mention of it in the book of Acts, nor has any incontrovertible evidence been found. Acts 2:10 and 11 mentions "visitors from Rome" who were present in Jerusalem on Pentecost to hear the first gospel proclamation. For some reason, Luke records there that these Romans included "both Jews and converts to Judaism." It is highly likely, then, that the gospel was first heard in Rome when these visitors (especially if they were among the 3000 baptized that day) returned to their homes and synagogues. This would explain why the church in Rome as late as A.D. 150 was worshiping in a manner similar to Jewish synagogues.[1] A commentary on Romans written under the name of

---

[1] Justin Martyr, *Apology I.*

Ambrosiastor around A.D. 380, probably in Rome, states that the Roman church arose among the Jews of Rome.[2]

We know from Acts 18:1-4 that Priscilla and Aquila, whom Paul greets in Romans 16:3 and 4, were in Corinth when Paul first arrived there because the Jews had been expelled from Rome by an edict of emperor Claudius. The Roman historian Suetonius says that this order was given because of a disturbance incited by one named Chrestus, likely a misspelling of Christus and a bit of a misunderstanding. Most probably, the preaching of the gospel of Christ had aroused such hostility among the Jews that they caused some civil disorder, which the emperor solved by banning them (or at least their leaders). They were allowed to return after Claudius's death four years later. Since this edict is dateable, we can be sure that by A.D. 49, the Christian faith was strong enough in Rome to cause trouble among non-Christian Jews.

So Paul is writing his epistle to a well-established community of Christians. The gospel has been at work among them for at least a decade and possibly as much as twenty-five years. The church was begun without direct help from an apostle and has continued to see things basically through Jewish eyes. At the same time, it seems that they have been quite successful in evangelizing Gentiles. Thus, the community Paul addresses is partly Jewish, partly Gentile, well established in the faith and in the knowledge of the Old Testament, but apparently suffering the stresses inherent in such a situation. Judging from Romans 14 and 15, there is, if not open strife, at least debate going on about the essentials of both Christian faith and Christian life, and to this debate Paul addresses himself.

The Form

Romans, as is true with the other writings of the apostle found in the New Testament, has the form of a letter. Just as our letters have a heading, a greeting, a body of information, and a closing signature, so first-century Greek letters had a four-part structure. The opening section identified the sender and the recipient and

---

[2]William Sanday and Arthur Headlam, *The Epistle to the Romans,* The International Critical Commentary (Edinburgh: T. & T. Clark, 1902), p. xxv.

included a greeting. The second part normally was a prayer of thanksgiving and blessing. Then followed the main body of the letter. It was closed with further greetings and often another prayer. A quick reading shows that Romans follows this pattern, but it is also clear that the body of the letter is quite long (1:13—15:13) and has an inner structure of its own. This section appears to be in the form of an essay with a formal opening, a logical progression, and application to life. Historians have found enough similar letter-essays from the first century to indicate that the form was not unheard of. Paul apparently adopted a recognizable way to teach and convince from a distance, and he obviously did it extremely well, since his epistles were protected, copied, and shared by their recipients.

The structure of the body of the letter seems to follow the logic of salvation, with the addition of a few passages (especially chapters 9—11) to deal with questions of special concern to the author and the recipients. He begins with the need of salvation—a vivid description of sinful humanity (1:18—3:20). He proceeds to proclaim the salvation worked out by God in the crucifixion of Jesus, which is made available to those who believe (3:21-31). He then discusses the nature of faith (chapter 4) and recapitulates his exposition (5:1-11). In Romans 5:12-21, he deals with the mystery of the cosmic conflict between sin and God as that conflict entered human history and was resolved in Christ. Chapter 6 looks at some of the implications of freedom from sin for the life of the Christian. Chapter 7 looks boldly at the possibility (some would say inescapability) of sin's ruling in even the Christian life. On the other hand, however, chapter 8 sounds the note of victory now and in God's future "for those who are in Christ Jesus."

In chapters 9, 10, and 11, Paul deals with several implications of questions he had raised in chapter 5 about the Jewish people and their relationship to God since Christ. Chapters 12—15 deal with how the Christian should live in the light of who he or she is by the grace of God.

All of this development is unified by the polemic contrasting salvation by law and by grace through faith. Thus, the words *righteousness* and *justification* appear often. They represent the same root word in Greek and are used by Paul both to teach what the gospel is and to show that it has nothing to do with the legalism of his former life in Pharisaism.

The Purpose

In scholarly circles, the big debate on Romans lately has centered on its purpose. For several centuries, it had been treated as a "compendium of the Christian religion,"[3] or at least a general survey of the theology of the apostle Paul.[4] But lately, people have begun to make connections between the epistle's content and a likely scenario in the Christian community in Rome.[5]

The purpose that the author states is to win the trust or friendship of the Roman Christians so that they will welcome him to Rome and help him on his next missionary thrust westward to Spain (Romans 1:10-15; 15:14-33). But the ethical teaching in chapters 14 and 15 is so specific that it forces the reader to consider a possible application in the Roman church. Chapter 16 shows that Paul had enough acquaintances in Rome that he could have known about serious tension between Jewish and non-Jewish members there. So it seems highly likely that in addition to his stated purpose, Paul also intends to help the Roman Christians over this hurdle with which he is already all too familiar. We can check this possibility as we move through our study of the book.

The Place of Romans in Church History

The book of Romans has played a dramatic role in the history of the church. Church history can be seen as a history of the interpretation of the Bible, so that the understanding of any Bible book has been from time to time crucial in that history. But Romans seems to have been involved in nearly every major turning point in the history of the church.

It is impossible to evaluate the impact Romans made on the early church. We know that by the end of the first century, Romans, along with other writings of the apostle Paul, was being copied and circulated generally among the churches. We know

---

[3]Phillip Melanchthon.

[4]Gunther Bornkamm has called it Paul's theological testament. *Geschichte und Glaube II* (Munchen: Chr. Kaiser Verlag, 1971), pp. 120-139.

[5]See *The Romans Debate,* ed. Karl P. Donfried (Minneapolis: Augsburg Publishing House, 1977).

that 2 Peter 3:15 and 16 refers to the writings of the apostle Paul, which were being twisted and misunderstood. We know that around A.D. 96, Clement of Rome quoted Paul's Roman letter as authoritative—most likely quoting from a single copy and not from a collection of Paul's letters. We know that about three years after the writing of the epistle, Paul was welcomed warmly to Rome by the Christians there (Acts 28:14, 15).

From these bits of information, we can deduce that the book was accepted from the beginning as an important and authoritative document, and within forty years was being copied and circulated as Scripture. The impact was certainly profound.

This importance has continued for more than 1900 years. The warning of 2 Peter 3:15 and 16 is illustrated clearly in the life of a man named Marcion, who around A.D. 140 made a list of New Testament documents that he accepted as authoritative. Romans and some other portions of Pauline books were on his list and, in fact, were used as criteria for judging the other books.

Marcion was a Gnostic, who tried to separate the gospel from the message of the Old Testament. The Gnostics held that God was perfect spirit and could have nothing to do with matter, which they saw as evil. Therefore, Marcion did not want to identify Yahweh, the Creator God of the Old Testament, with the Lord God of Jesus. Marcion was disfellowshiped by the Roman church for heresy; but his attempt to judge the content of the whole Bible by what he read in Romans shows the power of the Roman epistle in the early church. In addition, the whole controversy influenced the church's process of canonization, which eventually produced a consensus about the authoritative books we now call the New Testament.

About 240 years later in Milan, a young man was wrestling with God by reading Romans—a man who was later to become a bishop and the most powerful voice of the church of his day and for some time later. His name was Augustine. Here is how he later described that experience:

> So I was speaking and weeping in the most bitter contrition of my heart, when, lo! I heard from a neighboring house a voice as of a boy or girl, I know not, chanting, and oft repeating, "Take up and read; Take up and read." Instantly, my countenance altered, I began to think most intently whether children were wont in any kind of

play to sing such words; nor could I remember ever to have heard the like. So checking the torrent of my tears, I arose; interpreting it to be no other than a command from God to open the book, and read the first chapter I should find. . . . Eagerly then I returned to the place where Alypius was sitting; for there I had laid the volume of the Apostle when I arose thence. I seized, opened, and in silence read that section on which my eyes first fell: Not in rioting and drunkenness, not in chambering and wantonness, not in strife and envying; but put ye on the Lord Jesus Christ, and make no provision for the flesh, in concupiscence. No further would I read; nor needed I: for instantly at the end of this sentence, by a light as it were of serenity infused into my heart, all the darkness of doubt vanished away.[6]

Then as the dawn was breaking at the close of what we call the dark ages, in the spring of 1515, the young seminary professor, Martin Luther, began a series of lectures on Romans. These lectures would continue for eighteen months and would exert a powerful influence on his own life and on subsequent church history. Here are his comments on the preparation he made for those lectures:

I greatly longed to understand Paul's epistle to the Romans and nothing stood in the way but that one expression, "the justice of God," because I took it to mean that justice whereby God is just and deals justly in punishing the unjust. My situation was that, although an impeccable monk, I stood before God as a sinner troubled in conscience, and I had no confidence that my merit would assuage him. Therefore I did not love a just and angry God, but rather hated and murmured against him. Yet I clung to the dear Paul and had a great yearning to know what he meant.

Night and day I pondered until I saw the connection between the justice of God and the statement that "the just shall live by his faith." Then I grasped that the justice of God is that righteousness by which through grace and sheer mercy God justifies us through faith. Thereupon I felt myself to be reborn and to have gone

---

6Augustine, *Confessions,* the end of book 8.

through the open doors into paradise. The whole of Scripture took on a new meaning, and whereas before the "justice of God" had filled me with hate, now it became to me inexpressibly sweet in greater love. This passage of Paul became to me a gate to heaven. . . .[7]

Later, as Luther prepared to publish his translation of the New Testament, he wrote this paragraph to begin a preface to Romans:

This epistle is in truth the most important document in the New Testament, the whole gospel in its purest expression. Not only is it well worth a Christian's while to know it word for word by heart, but also to meditate on it day by day. It is the soul's daily bread, and can never be read too often or studied too much. The more you probe into it the more precious it becomes, and the better its flavour.[8]

Over 200 years later, in a small Moravian chapel in Aldersgate Street, London, the words of that preface were to change the life of young John Wesley and through him the religious complexion of England and America. It was May, 1738. Wesley had spent several years with very little success trying to evangelize the American Indians in Georgia. He returned to England very discouraged and conscious that something was lacking. Here is his report:

In the evening I went very unwillingly to a society in Aldersgate Street, where one was reading Luther's preface to the *Epistle to the Romans.* About a quarter of nine, while he was describing the change which God works in the heart through faith in Christ, I felt my heart strangely warmed. I felt I did trust in Christ, Christ alone for my salvation; and an assurance was given me that he had taken away my sins, even mine, and saved me from the law of sin and of death.[9]

---

[7]Cited in Roland Bainton, *Here I Stand* (New York: The New American Library of World Literature, 1950), pp. 49, 50.

[8]Cited in John Dillenberger, *Martin Luther* (Garden City: Doubleday & Co., 1961), p. 19.

[9]*The Journal of John Wesley* (Chicago: Moody Press, n. d.), p. 64.

Less than a hundred years had passed before a young preacher named Alexander Campbell preached a sermon on Romans 9—11 to a meeting of the Redstone Baptist Association at Cross Creek, Virginia, on August 30, 1816. This sermon clearly defined the difference between the authority of the Old Testament and that of the New Testament on the Christian. Thus was precipitated a movement of believers on the American continent which, 170 years later, has produced thousands of congregations of people known variously as Christian Churches, Churches of Christ, and Disciples of Christ.

The history of the church in the twentieth century continues to be punctuated by contact with Romans. In 1916, when theological liberalism had reached its zenith and when Europe was being shocked by the first world war, Karl Barth published his commentary on Romans, which, as has often been said, landed like a bombshell on the theological playground of Europe. It turned theological thinking around with a call to take the Bible seriously once again. In his preface to the second edition, which is the edition translated into English, he replies to his critics in these words:

> When I am named "Biblicist," all that can rightly be proved against me is that I am prejudiced in supposing the Bible to be a good book, and that I hold it to be profitable for men to take its conceptions at least as seriously as they take their own.[10]

In the second half of the century, C. K. Barrett, an outstanding British New Testament scholar, wrote: "Barth's commentary I read as an undergraduate. If in those days, and since, I remained and have continued to be a Christian, I owe the fact in large measure to that book."[11]

One might think that after all these years and all these outstanding scholars there would be nothing left to say about Romans. But

---

[10]Karl Barth, *The Epistle to the Romans,* trans. Edwyn Hoskins (London: Oxford University Press, 1933, reprint 1975), p. 12.

[11]C. K. Barrett, *A Commentary on the Epistle to the Romans* (London: Adam & Charles Black, 1973), p. vi.

it is nearly impossible to keep up with the scholarly, devotional, and sermonic output on the epistle. It continues to correct and instruct us at the end of the twentieth century, and it will obviously do so until the Lord's return.

CHAPTER ONE

The Gospel Introduced

Romans 1:1-17

The Greek letter writer customarily begins the salutation of a letter by identifying him or herself and then the person or group to which the letter is addressed. Paul's salutation in Romans is longer than usual, since he has not previously visited the Roman Christians and thus feels obliged to describe both himself and his opinion of them rather extensively.

Paul describes himself in three ways. First he calls himself "a servant of Christ Jesus." This, of course, emphasizes his relationship to Christ as slave to master, a relationship that is shared by every believer who submits to the lordship of Christ. Second, he claims that he was "called to be an apostle." The term *called* would for him and other believers mean not his reputation but the divine claim on his life. The word *apostle* indicates that the divine claim on him included a sending—a commission. The designation *apostle* would also elicit respect and, if accepted, go a long way toward opening the Roman Christians to Paul and his leadership.

The third element in Paul's self-description gives him the opportunity to make a preliminary statement of his faith and of his understanding of his mission. He says he has been "set apart for the gospel of God." His terminology here makes it likely that he is using a play on words to contrast his former life as a Pharisee, one who set himself apart from unrighteousness, and his present status as one set apart by God for the proclamation of God's righteousness to the unrighteous.

Romans 1:3-6 describes this gospel of God and introduces several concepts and activities that Paul will enlarge upon later. God's good news, he writes, is rooted in the history of God's dealing with people—it was "promised beforehand through his prophets in the Holy Scriptures" (Romans 1:2). And it announces an event of history, since it is "regarding his Son, who . . . was a descendant of David" (Romans 1:3). The Son of God is viewed in two aspects here: according to the flesh and according to the spirit. Paul will examine later in some detail life according to the flesh and according to the spirit. (See chapters 7 and 8.) Here his focus is on Christ, whose assumption of flesh put him in the lineage of David.

Christ was not only born, as all humans are; He also experienced the other universal human event: death. And in the throes of that most human experience, Paul indicates, God intervened "through the Spirit of holiness ... with power" to declare this dead man to be the Son of God "by his resurrection from the dead" (Romans 1:4). Having summarized the facts of the gospel, Paul now makes his ultimate confession of faith. This son of David/Son of God, dead and alive again, wears the name Jesus, bears the title Christ (Messiah), and occupies the position of Lord—specifically, *our* Lord. The most important thing Paul has in common with the Roman Christians is his and their confession of, and submission to, Jesus Christ as Lord.

The implications of this confession are summarized in verses 5 and 6. Paul has "received grace and apostleship." We usually connect grace to salvation, and of course Paul makes that connection very clear in other texts. But here his emphasis (as is true in Ephesians 3:2-11) is on God's grace in commissioning him to be a proclaimer of the gospel. His specific purpose is "to call people from among all the Gentiles to the obedience that comes from faith" (Romans 1:5). This mention of (literally) "obedience of faith," which is repeated in Romans 16:26 and in slightly different form in Romans 15:18, is too often overlooked in controversies over "works righteousness" and "faith only." Paul seems to indicate here that some act of obedience is to be expected from people who submit to the lordship of Christ. After all, a lord is by definition one who is to be obeyed. The age-old controversy over this question has been a problem of our interpretation of Paul and James, and not one inherent in the New Testament.

Paul identifies his readers by first reminding them, in Romans 1:6, of how the Lordship of Christ has affected their lives. He sees them as being among the Gentiles who have become obedient believers and thus among the called ones (the elect) of Jesus Christ.

In verse 7, he continues this description of his readers, locating them in Rome, the capital of the most powerful empire on earth, and describing them as "loved by God and called to be saints." He could hardly have complimented them more highly than to place them within the saving love of God and to designate them as recipients of God's holiness.

His greeting to them is simple and yet profound: "grace and peace." The Greek word translated "grace" was the normal greeting (although in another form) for the people of that language and era. Yet Paul used it to describe the unmerited love of God for humankind; so it can hardly be read as a customary greeting. His yoking grace with peace adds further weight to the theological content here. *Peace* is the equivalent of the familiar Hebrew term *shalom* (which was used by the Jews as a greeting). This word refers far beyond the absence of conflict to the peace with God that we call salvation. So the grace and peace that Paul wishes for the Roman Christians is available only "from God our Father and from the Lord Jesus Christ" (Romans 1:7).

In the next three verses, Paul summarizes the content of his prayers in reference to these believers in Rome—prayers of thanksgiving, intercession, and petition. He mentions one specific reason for his gratitude for them all—their "faith is being reported all over the world" (Romans 1:8). Paul had apparently heard much about the church in Rome during his travels around the empire. Their renown centered on their faith. Since faith becomes such a big issue in the epistle and since this is the first time Paul uses the term by itself (in verse 5, he mentions the obedience of faith), we should note here that the word translated "faith" or "belief" could also be translated "faithfulness" or "loyalty." In fact, in the Greek versions of the Old Testament, the word usually has the latter meaning, quite often referring to the faithfulness of God himself. Since Luther's breakthrough, mentioned in the introduction, most translators have preferred "faith." I bring this up here to indicate that the term *faith* refers to more than an act of the mind. It points to a condition of total dedication—of following the Lord no matter what.

The second aspect of Paul's prayer is his constant intercession for them. He specifies no definite need here, only that he remembers them in his prayers. His petition, on the other hand, is very specific. He wants to visit them and so prays for this to become possible.

Verses 11-15 give us several reasons for his wanting to go to Rome. He states first of all his desire to "impart ... some spiritual gift to make [them] strong" (Romans 1:11). Paul's status as an apostle presumably empowered him to help Christians by means of special manifestations of the power of the Holy Spirit. (See Romans 15:19.) Precisely what he intends here is not stated; perhaps he is not clear about it himself. But he hurries on, in verse 12, to correct any hint of arrogance on his part by restating his desire in terms of mutual encouragement, emphasizing the fact that any believer can and should be a blessing to any other believer with whom he or she has contact.

Another purpose for Paul's visit to Rome—a visit often planned but until now prevented—was evangelism. Paul's mention of having a "harvest" among them is clearly a statement of his desire to preach the gospel in Rome, not only to the believers but also to unbelievers. Paul's motivation for evangelism in Rome is not that Rome needed the gospel worse than other places, but that he understands himself to be "obligated both to Greeks and non-Greeks, both to the wise and the foolish" (Romans 1:14). His commission is to preach the gospel to persons regardless of race, nationality, culture, philosophy, or education. As he will explain in chapter 15, Rome is the next logical step in his itinerary, and as we can imagine, it would be an important, strategic location for further westward expansion, especially since there is already a strong Christian community there.

This brings us to one of the best known statements in the Bible—verse 16. In fact, verses 16 and 17 should always be read together. The statement is a natural outgrowth of what comes before, but it also stands as a sort of thesis statement for the development of the thought of the rest of the epistle. It begins with a simple, personal affirmation, "I am not ashamed of the gospel." Since shame is a negative reaction, this can be read as a sort of double-negative (therefore positive) understatement. But in light of what we know about the temptation to reject, or at least hide, one's Christian commitment—a temptation that has not disappeared—we should recognize that Paul is pointing to his continuing willingness to risk all for the gospel.

Why would a person run such a risk? "Because it is the power of God for the salvation of everyone who believes," and in it "a righteousness from God is revealed." A full discussion of the meaning of *righteousness* must wait until we reach chapter 4. But it is important here to consider this word *gospel*. Most people who have been Christians for a year or more are aware that the term *gospel* means good news. But what is often overlooked is the fact that the word is nearly exclusively found in Paul's writings. It appears, in one of four forms, eighty-four times in Pauline literature, while being used only seventy times in the rest of the New Testament and the early church fathers' writings. In Galatians 1 and 2, Paul treats the gospel as an identifiable body of teaching that can be contrasted to "another gospel" or no gospel at all. In 1 Corinthians 15, he defines *gospel* in terms of the facts of Jesus' death, burial, resurrection, and appearances. Here in Romans, he describes it as power for salvation and as a vehicle for God's self-revelation.

It is obvious that Paul's use of the word *gospel* includes the whole scope of his life as a Christian. It refers to his own experience of conversion and commission on the road to Damascus. It embraces all the new historical and doctrinal thinking he had to do as a result of that event. It points to the reality of Jesus as the dominant fact of all history. It defines Paul's own lifework as a missionary. And it describes the results of his preaching, not only in terms of the conversion of individuals, but also as the fulfillment of the expectation of the whole Old Testament that the kingdom or covenant of God would be opened to all the nations of the earth. Paul's good news is that in Christ, God's promise to Abraham (Genesis 18:18 and 22:18) is being fulfilled—the promise that all the nations of the earth would be blessed through Abraham's offspring. This helps to explain why Paul so often repeats the phrases "first for the Jew, then for the Gentile" (Romans 1:16). Paul, without arrogance, sees himself as the major proclaimer of this good news to the nations.

As mentioned earlier, we should postpone our attempt to understand fully Paul's use of *righteousness* until we have reached at least chapter 4; but verse 17 presents us with our first major problem of translation and interpretation. What the New International Version renders "a righteousness that is by faith from first to last" reads literally (as the translators admit in a footnote) "from faith to faith." Most translators and commentators understand this phrase to be Paul's way of saying what Martin Luther made explicit in his phrase "by faith alone." But keeping in mind the primary Old Testament meaning of faith as faithfulness and as often referring to God (see Romans 3:3), we could also translate it "from [God's] faithfulness to [our] faith." This is, after all, the direction of the gospel and the actual wording of the sentence.

The passage closes with the quotation from Habakkuk 2:4, "The righteous will live by faith." Paul has seen fit to leave a pronoun out of his quotation of this verse, which in Hebrew states that the righteous will live by his own faith or faithfulness, and in the Greek translation (the Septuagint) says that the righteous shall live by God's faithfulness or by faith in God (the pronoun there is "my"). The way Paul quotes it here lays that question of interpretation aside and leaves the statement general enough to stand as a text for the rest of the book. Actually, as it stands, it could be translated, "He who is righteous by faith will live." This translation is even a good outline of the rest of the epistle, chapters 1—11 showing how a person becomes righteous by faith and chapters 12—15 dealing with how to live on that basis.

Paul's introduction of the gospel in these verses makes two dominant points: it is the gospel of God and it is the gospel for us.

It is, first of all, God's gospel (Romans 1:1), since God is the only one who could make really good news possible. And He did. As God's good news, the gospel is the revelation of God (Romans 1:17). It was not what people were expecting. Both Jews and Gentiles were caught off guard by the proclamation of Jesus Christ. It was not a message of philosophy or human wisdom. In fact, as Paul writes in 1 Corinthians 1 and 2, it was laughed at as foolishness by those who sought wisdom. It was not a new list of legal demands. Christ's teaching and His crucifixion caused somewhat of a crisis in connection with the law. It was actually a new view of God himself—a God of righteousness who takes the seemingly unrighteous step of justifying the wicked (Romans 4:5).

As God's good news, the gospel is the Son of God (Romans 1:9). It is not a book of deep thinking, as important as that can be. It is not a list of instructions, as much as we need that. It is not even just a good example, since it centers on the incarnate God, a status none of us can attain. The gospel is the life, death, and resurrection of Jesus Christ our Lord. Our thinking about Him is important. His teachings for us are important. Our aspiring to live as He did is important. But most important is what He has done for our salvation, which we could not have accomplished for ourselves.

As God's good news, the gospel is the purpose of God (Romans 1:5). By this I mean not only that the gospel reveals God's will, but also that it is the major instrument for the accomplishment of that gracious will. God's purpose is not limited; the gospel is for everybody—both Jews and Greeks. In the gospel, God's redemption is offered, which means that the gospel is designed to awaken faith—the acceptance of the truth of the good news, which is necessary for the reception of that redemption. The new reality of faith lives and grows in the process of obedience to the continual hearing of the gospel. (See Romans 12:1, 2.) Thus, the purpose of God seems to be, for the present, totally tied to the gospel.

As God's good news, the gospel is the power of God (Romans 1:16). We too often denigrate words as being weak. "That's just talk," we say; or, "Talk is cheap." But God's talk created the universe; so His message does not consist of weak words. The powerful word of the resurrection, by which God's Spirit declared Jesus to be the Son of God, is the same power that accomplishes the salvation of every believer.

So we see that the gospel is wholly God's; but Paul can also call it "my gospel" (Romans 2:16). It is the good news of God for us. Paul will make what is for us Christians an almost commonplace statement in Romans 4:25, "He was delivered over to death for our sins." *Redemption, salvation, atonement, reconciliation,* and—for Paul the greatest of such words—*justification,* are all terms that indicate that we human beings are in a bad way and cannot improve our lot without God's help. In other words, from our standpoint, any consideration of the gospel must begin with the awareness of sin. As we shall see in the next chapter, that is just where Paul begins. The gospel is for our sins.

God's good news is for us also because it is given for our hearing. It is put in our human language. Now that is a risky business, as we all know who have misunderstood and been misunderstood even in communication with those who are closest to us. But God is consistent. He made salvation possible by becoming one of us, and He makes salvation available by offering it in human language. Furthermore, the form of that language is not just propositions or explanations or rules or reprimands; it is basically the story of Jesus—language that goes beyond the intellect to the heart.

God's good news is for us also because He sends it for the obedience of our faith. The response God expects from those who really hear His gospel is the belief that is accompanied by obedience of the Lord. The usual initial act of obedience is immersion in water, the meaning of which Paul discusses in Romans 6:1-14. Since the expected response to the gospel is neither doctrinal, technical, nor physically demanding, it is possible for all of us. When we witness the baptism of a person with severe mental or physical handicaps and note that she or he is at least as thrilled as would be a "normal" person, we are struck by the importance of this aspect of the gospel. It should cause us to praise God for His great mercy. An aspect closely related to this is the fact that the gospel is not forced on anybody. It is offered to us all in terms to which we can relate, and we are left to make the decision of faith.

God's good news is also for our salvation. As we shall see (especially in Romans 5:1-11), this means more than the future deliverance of our souls from God's wrath, although that is also included. But God's gospel heals life in its totality. It offers security, encouragement, hope, and meaning for life—here and hereafter.

God's good news is also for our proclamation. This is perhaps the most surprising and frightening aspect of the gospel. God runs the risk of entrusting the gospel to us—to the very sinners who needed it in the first place. This points not only to the general risk of putting the message in human language, but to the specific risk (one we know only too well) of leaving it to you and me, of all people, to communicate it. And, as someone has said, as far as we know, God has no Plan B. Thus, the church is always just one generation from extinction. As foolish as that may seem (see 1 Corinthians 1:21), it has worked more or less effectively for nearly two thousand years. Since the days of Peter and Paul, God has used very unpromising people to accomplish great things. We believe that He is still capable of doing that and is, in fact, doing it. He needs only our willingness—our cooperation—to tell His story to the best of our ability.

God has made His gospel so that we in turn can pass it on to others.

CHAPTER TWO

The Need for the Gospel

Romans 1:18—2:29

The first step in presenting the gospel is to convince the hearer that he or she needs it. So Paul begins his exposition of the gospel of salvation by looking at the wrath of God and the sins of humans that call it forth. In Romans 1:17, he has claimed that in the gospel "a righteousness from God is revealed." In verse 18, something else is revealed: the wrath of God. This appears to be a rather harsh contrast; but without the understanding of the grace of God, which we gain from the gospel, it would likely seem natural to us to begin a consideration of the nature of God with His wrath. The chief Roman god, Jupiter, was god of the storm. Much pagan religious practice was devoted to placating the gods and escaping the destruction of their wrath.

Of course, Paul quickly points out that God's wrath is not arbitrary. It is revealed "against all the godlessness and wickedness of [persons] who suppress the truth by their wickedness" (Romans 1:18). Just what he means by this is explained in the next several verses. First, he points out that they should have known about the true God, since He has made it possible for everybody to know something about Him. What can be known? God's "eternal power and divine nature" (Romans 1:20). How can this be known? "From what has been made"—literally "by the works," a statement that, similarly to Psalm 103:22, sees God's works in creation as speaking. And so what? This is not just idle speculation, not what some would call natural theology. The reason Paul begins with a revelation of God available to everybody is to point out that everybody is "without excuse." Nobody can plead innocence. We all experience the creation in which we live, and this should stimulate us to seek its Creator.

Verses 21-23 define, in Paul's words, the basic sin of humanity: idolatry. He explains that this act of rebellion begins negatively:

idolatry

"they neither glorified him as God nor gave thanks to him" (Romans 1:21). This refusal to worship the true God led to a futility of thinking and to a darkening of the heart. Thus, both reason and will are damaged. This lays the foundation for the peculiar conflict between the concept of wisdom common to sinful human beings and the true divine wisdom that shows our brand to be foolish. He develops this contrast further in 1 Corinthians 1 and 2. The final step in this process of sin is the actual development of idol worship. It seems true that, as Bob Dylan's song puts it, "You've gotta serve somebody." It is not that people go around consciously seeking an object of worship, but we simply cannot be objective and detached about everything around us. If we refuse to glorify the Creator, we seem bound to exchange the glory of the immortal God for images of something around us. Worship is not bad; in fact, it is inescapable. But to worship anything or any person other than God is to focus on something secondary instead of primary, something finite instead of infinite, something made instead of its Maker. This accords ultimate status to something less than ultimate, which obviously misses the mark completely.

This description of the origin of sin is not peculiar to Paul. One can easily recognize that it is basically the same description found in the Old Testament. The words are similar to those in Psalm 106:20, Jeremiah 2:11, and Deuteronomy 4:15-18. But perhaps most important is the parallel with Genesis 1:20ff. There, the very creatures Paul lists in Romans 1:23 as objects of humankind's distorted worship are listed as works of God. It is especially important to note that several of these Old Testament texts identify such idols as Israel's problem. Thus, Paul is not just condemning the Gentiles here (although a legalistic Jew might take his words that way), but he is describing the basis for the sin of all human beings.

The rest of the chapter reads like a catalog of sins. But if we catch the import of the refrain, "God gave them over," which appears in verses 24, 26, and 28, we notice that the basic sin is still idolatry, as Paul reiterates in verse 25. The rest of the transgressions are listed as punishments for sin—or, at least, results of sin. It is hardly necessary to comment on the details here. Our English versions translate Paul's lists graphically enough for us to recognize what he is saying. Sexual immorality and murder are listed alongside greed, gossip, and disobedience of parents, with no distinction noted. All of these acts and attitudes are seen as unnatural—as going against the will of God, by which we humans and the universe in which we live are created. And the whole mess is traceable to the rebellious refusal to glorify God as Creator.

The picture is ludicrous: finite creatures standing on our hind legs, looking at the wondrous intricacies of the universe and deciding to pretend that there is no Creator. The sham gets even more tragic when we realize that we need something to worship; so we form objects or develop organizations or exalt heroes or write philosophies or engineer experiences to control us. We declare our independence from the loving Creator to submit to something no greater than ourselves.

Each age, of course, has invented its own terminology for what J. B. Phillips called "deliberate atheism." In the first two-thirds of the twentieth century, the term was *science*. Both theists and atheists contributed to what was seen as a conflict of science and religion. We like to put such matters in these absolute terms. But what we actually had was conflict within and among some people who found security in scientism and others who found it in religiosity. The religionists involved in the conflict never knew quite what to do with reports like the one still circulating in Princeton, New Jersey, of Albert Einstein standing in his backyard watching an eclipse of the moon with an expression of childlike awe on his face. Scientism folks could hardly cope with believers who admitted that the medieval church had been wrong about Copernicus and Galileo and that we might even be misunderstanding our own Bible at some points.

Regardless of what some people think, such a form of "deliberate atheism"—and the resultant conflicts—are ancient history now. Our generation has come up with a new format for rejecting the Creator. It is called (among other terms) "liberationism." Just as with science, there is nothing inherently wrong with the word *liberation* or its meaning. But when it becomes an "ism"—an end in itself—it faces two problems. It has lost its reason for being (to free people from oppression), and it has supplanted the connection with the One who created us free in the first place. We are again running the risk of falling into the trap of the ancients whom Paul has described in this passage.

Is it any wonder, then, that Paul warns his readers, in Rome or wherever we live, that this kind of action is bound to awaken God's wrath? The wrath of God is not His meanness, or, as the

31

New English Bible translates it, "divine retribution." It is, in Phillips' words, "the holy anger of God." God's righteousness has two sides: His gracious love and His holy anger. If God never reacted against evil, He could hardly be called good. Furthermore, we could hardly talk about His loving us if He were not disappointed when we reject Him. So just as our freedom includes the ability to choose evil, so God's freedom includes the wrath against all ungodliness and wickedness.

We should, then, be aware that God takes us very seriously, which means that He takes our sin very seriously. We are dealing with no wishy-washy divinity. We are dealing with the almighty, righteous Lord of creation, who has made us capable of using our heads and our hearts in His service. We are dealing with the gracious Lord of eternity, who has given His only-begotten Son to reconcile us to himself. We are dealing with the One before whom we shall stand and answer for our decisions. God takes us very seriously; we had better take Him seriously as our Lord, our Savior, and our Judge.

As we read on into chapter 2, we see Paul narrowing his focus somewhat. Romans 1:18-32 has shown sin to be in the background and experience of all of us. But there are always those who are ready to "pass judgment on someone else" (Romans 2:1). It is on these people that Paul turns the spotlight of the gospel in Romans 2:1-11. If there is only one basic sin, and if everybody does it, then all sin's symptoms—all of what we call sins—are equally damaging, since they all show that the perpetrator is out of touch with God. Thus, Paul has good reason to remind people that "at whatever point you judge the other, you are condemning yourself, because you who pass judgment do the same things" (Romans 2:1).

The apostle is not much concerned about the social or psychological results of the sin of judging; he goes right to the heart of the matter. He warns that such an attitude puts persons in danger of God's judgment. These eleven verses are structured on a contrast between God and human beings. The term *man* here (Romans 2:3) is the generic word for human individual *(anthropos)* and does not refer to gender. So we should read this analysis as referring to both men and women.

The human judge is first warned of the danger of God's judgment (Romans 2:3). Second, such judging shows "contempt for the riches of his kindness, tolerance and patience" (Romans 2:4).

32

And third, Paul says that such human judgment displays "your stubbornness and your unrepentant heart," which only prepares for "the day of God's wrath" (Romans 2:5).

On the other hand, "God's judgment ... is based on truth" (Romans 2:2). God is a judge whose "kindness leads you toward repentance" (Romans 2:4). God's judgment is "righteous" (Romans 2:5). Then, beginning with verse 6, Paul concentrates on this righteous judgment of God, introducing his analysis by quoting Psalm 62:12 and Proverbs 24:12: "God will give to each person according to what he has done" (Romans 2:6).

We should remind ourselves at this point where we are in Paul's presentation. He has not yet begun to deal with the reality of God's grace in Christ. He is continuing his description of the universality and effect of sin. He is explaining here the wrath of God under which all of us who are separate from Christ fall.

Romans 2:7-10 forms what is called a "chiasmus," a statement structured in such a way that the second half is a sort of mirror image of the first. Paul begins and ends with the positive (Romans 2:7, 10) and deals with the negative in the middle (Romans 2:8, 9). The structure can be symbolized as A B; B A, with the hinge coming where Paul says, "There will be wrath and anger. There will be trouble and distress." This indicates the care with which Paul worked as he put the very important statements of his epistle into writing. Thus, he makes clear here that under the dispensation of God's righteous wrath, eternal salvation is possible only for "those who by persistence in doing good seek glory, honor and immortality" (Romans 2:7). He summarizes this with the simple statement, "For God does not show favoritism" (Romans 2:11).

Paul then draws some implications from his premises of universal revelation and God's justice (Romans 2:12, 13). Since there is no ignorance, everybody will be judged. Since God is just, His judgment will use the criteria of the person being judged. For those under the Old Testament law, judgment will be based on whether or not that law was kept. For those apart from that law, the Mosaic law will not be a factor. In either case, a person's deserving salvation depends on that person's obeying law, not just hearing it.

Verses 14 and 15 appear as a kind of interruption of the flow of thought, but an important interruption. Paul seems to have come nearly to the end of this exposition of the universality of sin, only to realize that he has not dealt directly with the nature of the law by which Gentiles will be judged. He first points out that some Gentiles, when they "do by nature things required by the law," demonstrate that the law can be kept. "They are a law for themselves ... since they show that the requirements of the law are written on their hearts." Cicero, the Roman stoic philosopher, wrote something similar: "The law is the supreme reason implanted in nature which approves the things that ought to be done, and prohibits what ought not to be done."[12] Here in Romans, Paul seems to be pulling together pagan philosophy, Jewish thinking[13], and his Christian understanding of the day of judgment. He ties the role of the conscience as accuser and defender with "the day when God will judge" (Romans 2:16).

Once again we are faced with the power of sin. Paul makes it clear that even though he must allow for the possibility of righteousness according to whatever law one has, he can in practice deal only negatively with such judgment, since the whole discussion follows the statement about sin and perishing in verse 12. And since these sixteen verses are directed to those who judge others, it is important for Paul to complete his thought with the reminder that God is the true judge, that He will judge through Jesus Christ, and that this is all clarified in the gospel.

At verse 17, Paul narrows the focus even more. He proceeds to use the very terms and claims that, as he well knows, are used by the children of Israel in his day. They are Jews, that is, of the family of Judah, one of Israel's sons. They rely on the law. They are proud of their special relationship with God. They claim to know God's will and to demonstrate superior living by knowing the law (Romans 2:18). They claim to be in a position to guide, enlighten, and teach the world (Romans 2:19, 20). Furthermore, as Paul is also aware, they have good reason for thinking of themselves in these ways. The trouble is that this self-image is based more on possession of the law than on obedience of it—more on certain rituals than on faith.

So in Romans 2:21-23, Paul reverses his description of the Jew and turns it into an accusation. He vividly shows the results of

---

[12]Cicero, *De Legibus,* 1.6.18.

[13]See Jeremiah 31:33 and the apocryphal passages, Wisdom of Solomon 7 and 9 and 1 Enoch 63:1-9.

their hypocrisy in the verse quoted from Isaiah 52:5 and Ezekiel 36:22, "God's name is blasphemed among the Gentiles because of you" (Romans 2:24). It is too easy to forget that added advantages bring added responsibilities.

The rest of chapter 2 concentrates on what the strict Jews themselves identified as the major sign of Jewishness: circumcision. This sign goes clear back to Abraham; so it is even more ancient and basic than the signs of the covenant law given through Moses or the covenant kingdom brought by David. Circumcision, Paul points out, is not the essence of the relationship with God, but its symbol. The essence is internal: "of the heart, by the Spirit" (Romans 2:29). This covenant is shown not only by the surgical act of circumcision, but also by the obvious acts of obedience (Romans 2:25-27). If obedience does not accompany circumcision, then the latter is canceled. The corollary also holds: the uncircumcised who obey the law may be "regarded as though they were circumcised" (Romans 2:26).

So even Jews at their best are sinners in need of forgiveness. This raises some questions with which Paul will deal in chapters 3 and 9—11, but for now he has made his point that all human beings are sinners and even under law are recipients only of the wrath of God. Sin, he has pointed out (Romans 1:18), is both against God and against God's order. His words are translated "godlessness" and "wickedness." These two aspects of sin are seen clearly in the rehearsed confession of the younger son in Jesus' parable, "I have sinned against heaven and against you." This son also knew the result of sin: "I am no longer worthy to be called your son" (Luke 15:18, 19). Sin, as rebellion against God and His will for human life, causes alienation on all levels.

If you are not a Christian, you might seem to have an advantage at this point. You might not be conscious of such alienation—which is, of course, an unreal advantage based on ignorance. But for us Christians, there always seems to be tension between God's grace and His wrath. This is why we have difficulty harmonizing Jesus' angry cleansing of the temple (Mark 11:15-17 and parallels) with our picture of Him as totally loving. We tend to idealize love so as to define it in terms of indifference to the negative aspects of life. But we know that we don't live that way. We are hurt most deeply by the sins of those we most love. In fact, the opposite of love is not anger, but indifference. God could be neither righteous nor loving if He did not react with wrath to the sins of His human creatures. Thus, it must be true, as Paul has structured his argument, that the wrath of God is one aspect of His righteousness, which is being revealed in the gospel.

There is one other topic presented in this section, which evangelical Christians rarely deal with: the importance of worship. We dare not overlook the basis of all sin—the refusal, in spite of all available revelation, to glorify God (Romans 1:21). Paul leaves no doubt about his commitment to evangelism and his concern for correct statements about the Christian faith. But we see both in his identification of the fundamental sin as idolatry and in his repeated (Romans 1:25 and often throughout the epistle) statements of spontaneous praise that he is convinced that worship is a natural result of faith and a vital part of the experience of the faithful.

As we shall see in chapters 3, 5, and 7, we are not yet finished with the topic of sin. But in Romans 1:18—2:29, Paul has laid the groundwork for the preaching of, and the hearing of, the gospel by demonstrating that all persons are equal in that all people sin and thus are worthy of no better than the wrath of God. This is but the beginning of the good news.

CHAPTER THREE

The Heart of the Gospel

Romans 3:1-31

Having demonstrated that "Jews and Gentiles alike are all under sin" (Romans 3:9), Paul's presentation of the gospel now reaches a transition. In this chapter, he accomplishes three things: he deals first with the question of whether or not there is any advantage to being a Jew (1-8); he then concludes his exposition of the universality of sin by quoting Scripture and pointing out the accountability of every person before God (9-20); he finally (21-31) gives us the first of a number of transitional passages (compare Romans 5:1-11; 8:1-4; 12:1, 2), which say so much in so few words that they leave the reader breathless!

"What advantage, then, is there in being a Jew?" (Romans 3:1). Tevye, the Jewish-Russian milkman in *Fiddler on the Roof,* asks a similar question in one of his many conversations with God. He complains, "I know the Jews are your chosen people, but couldn't you choose somebody else for a change?"[14] With all the trouble the Jews have had in the world, it seems sometimes that their special relationship to the Lord is their only advantage. And Paul has apparently taken that away by demonstrating that they are just as much in need of divine forgiveness as are the Gentiles.

---

[14]This is similar to the lament quoted by William Bausch, *Storytelling: Imagination and Faith* (Mystic, CT: Twenty-Third Publications, 1984), pp. 66f, from a victim of Hitler's persecution: "Lord, four thousand years ago, on the slopes of Mount Sinai, you chose the Jews as a people peculiar unto you, a holy people, a nation of priests, to bear the yoke of your holy Law and to serve as witness to all the world. Lord, I am deeply sensible of the honor, but Lord, enough is enough. Surely it is time you chose somebody else."

Paul, however, will not allow that he has ruled out advantage. He has merely pointed out that advantage brings responsibility. In the latter part of Romans 3:2, it appears that Paul is beginning a list of advantages, but the rest of the list is missing—or at least postponed for a while. Actually he returns to it in Romans 9:4, 5. At this point, it is sufficient to point out that the descendants of Abraham have been the primary vessel of God's self-revelation. "They have been entrusted with the very words of God" (Romans 3:2).

Now the possession of the oracles of God is a great privilege, but it is obviously no guarantee of salvation. As Paul will later say, hearing the word is what produces faith (Romans 10:17), not just having it. Romans 3:3 points out that in spite of having the Word, some have not come to faith. Here it becomes clear why Paul is so concerned with this question of Jewish status. It is not just an academic concern for the nature of Judaism or of faith. It goes directly to the nature of God himself. "Will their lack of faith nullify God's faithfulness?" (Romans 3:3). Keep in mind here that the same Greek word is translated both "faith" (belief) and "faithfulness" (loyalty). The faithfulness of God to His covenant promises—in other words, God's truth and trustworthiness—is not to be doubted. So Paul replies to the question with his characteristic strong negative expletive, which the NIV translates, "Not at all!" (Romans 3:4). "WRONG!" he shouts; "NO WAY!" God by definition—no, by nature—is true, faithful, and righteous. For Paul and his hearers in Rome, all the evidence one needs for this is a Biblical word, which he offers from Psalm 51:4. This Psalm is very appropriate, since it deals with the utter sinfulness of a human being and glorifies God in it.

But the conversation is not over. Paul continues to reason with his readers in the same way the Jewish rabbis reasoned with one another—in question-and-answer style. The three questions in verses 5-8 are closely related and follow a line of perverse logic, focusing on a possible positive result of sin. As darkness makes one appreciate the light, perhaps "our unrighteousness brings out God's righteousness more clearly." Does that mean "that God is unjust in bringing his wrath on us?" (Romans 3:5). In a similar vein, why should I be punished for acts of falsehood that glorify God by enhancing His own truthfulness? (See Romans 3:7.) And then comes the ultimate absurdity, "Let us do evil that good may result" (Romans 5:8). All three of these possibilities are rejected forcefully. In verse 6, Paul employs again, as in verse 4, his strong negation, following it with the reminder that God is the world's judge, which implies that His criteria cannot be so relativized. The final statement is so absurd that Paul merely dismisses those who accuse him of teaching such things: "Their condemnation is deserved."

Such reasoning as Paul caricatures here seems ridiculous when looked at in print, but it is not so uncommon as we might think. The person wanting to justify non-Christian behavior often resorts to such thinking. Even the familiar, "After all, I'm only human," has theological implications, since it indicates something fundamentally wrong with the way God made us. At base, these are all ways to shift the responsibility for sin to God himself. This escape Paul will not permit.

The next section (Romans 3:9-20) forms the conclusion of Paul's contention that every person is a sinner, whether Jew or Gentile. "All are under sin" (Romans 3:9). Oddly enough, this is the first time Paul uses the noun *sin* in the epistle. As we shall see, especially in chapters 5 and 7, he treats sin as a sort of personal power of evil, not just as the sum of human transgressions. And so, here he pictures sin as, in some sense, being in charge—in the driver's seat, we might say. We sinners are "under sin," or at its mercy. But, of course, that does not relieve us from responsibility; it just paints the picture of our status in the darkest possible colors.

Verses 10-18 are composed of a chain *(catena)* of Old Testament statements, of which all but one (Isaiah 59:7, 8) are from what the Jews call the "Writings." These are from various Psalms and Ecclesiastes 7:30. The reader should refer to the original contexts, as noted in footnotes or marginal references in most of our versions of the Bible. Each verse quoted emphasizes the grip sin has on the human race; and in vivid terms, they describe the results of sin.

All that is left for Paul to do after these quotations is to make the point of individual accountability, and this he does in Romans 3:19 and 20. Since it is already clear that pagans had to make a radical change (to repent) in order to obtain God's forgiveness, it is necessary only to demonstrate that the same holds true for Jews—those under the law. It should be noted here that Paul differentiates between being under sin (Romans 3:9) and under the law (Romans 3:19) by using two different prepositions,

39

although the distinction is hard to express in English. The New English Bible comes close when it translates the first phrase "under the power of sin," and the second, "within the pale of the law." Even the divine law is not an escape from sin; rather, it is an accusation of sin. Its final effect is "that every mouth may be silenced and the whole world held accountable to God" (Romans 3:19). What the law accomplishes, then, is that through it "we become conscious of sin" (Romans 3:20).

Romans 3:21 begins what we usually think of as the gospel—God's good news. Paul has argued convincingly the universality of sin and shown that even the law of God—at least, as it is usually taught and applied—only increases our awareness of sin. Now he will explain what he had in mind in Romans 1:17, when he put together the terms *righteousness* and *faith*.

In Romans 1:18, he began his exposition of the revelation of God's righteousness with the revelation of His wrath. In Romans 3:21, he arrives at the positive side of this revelation: "a righteousness from God, apart from law, has been made known." Since we usually understand righteousness as a quality we attain by will and discipline, and since we need rules, or at least standards to aim for, in order to be righteous, it might seem contradictory to us to talk about righteousness apart from, or independent of, law. So it must have seemed to Paul's Roman readers: Jews, whose very definition of righteousness was found in the *Torah*—the law of the Old Testament—and other citizens of Rome, whose way of life (the *pax Romana)* was established and guarded by law and order. Yet Paul has just shown how people in neither group really live by the law they are under.

The first thing Paul says about this righteousness is that it was testified to by the Law and the Prophets. In other words, God's previous revelation is not irrelevant. It should, however, be read as pointing to the gospel. The second thing we should know about this righteousness is the means God used to accomplish it. The first part of Romans 3:22 can be translated two different ways, but the one that seems to make most sense points to God's means, Jesus Christ. Most versions read something like the New International Version: "This righteousness from God comes through faith in Jesus Christ to all who believe." Those last nine words seem strangely redundant. A literal translation, however, using the word *faithfulness* (see above, pages 24, 25, 38) in the first phrase makes good sense: "But God's righteousness [is available]

40

by means of the faithfulness of Jesus Christ, unto all who believe." Reading it in this way, we see that it points to Jesus as the one who actually accomplished the new righteousness of God apart from law, and it still states clearly Paul's third point—that we are to receive righteousness by faith instead of attaining it by works of law.

The importance of this proclamation is underscored as Paul, in verses 23 and 24, reiterates it in other words. As many versions recognize, he actually begins with the final clause of verse 22, "There is no difference. . . ." In this reiteration, Paul introduces three concepts not mentioned earlier. First, he describes sinners as those who "fall short of the glory of God" (Romans 3:23). The term translated "fall short" could just as well be rendered "lack." In Jewish thinking, the glory of God was not just a characteristic of God, but also a quality originally possessed by Adam and Eve but lost by them as a result of sin. In the first-century Jewish document *The Life of Adam and Eve,* we read that Eve, having eaten of the forbidden fruit, said to the serpent, "Why have you done this to me, that I have been estranged from my glory with which I was clothed?" This narrative continues with Adam's fall and his statement to Eve, which ends, "You have estranged me from the glory of God."[15] So Paul and his Jewish contemporaries, among whom were some of the Roman Christians, understood lacking the glory of God as a result of sin from the time of Eve and Adam's very first act of disobedience. Sin attacks the very essence of our creation.

Second, Paul identifies for the first time in this letter God's justification as a gift coming from grace. In Romans 3:24, we discover the heart of Paul's special emphasis: justification by grace.[16] This verse consists of only twelve words in the original language, but in those words, Paul makes his point at least five different ways. First, he uses a passive verb form, in contrast to the previous verse: "All sinned and lack . . . being justified." No

[15]James Charlesworth, ed., *The Old Testament Pseudepigrapha,* Vol. 2, "Life of Adam and Eve," translated by M. D. Johnson (Garden City, N. Y.: Doubleday & Company, 1985), p. 281.

[16]The word appears 100 times in the Pauline literature (24 times in Romans alone) and only 55 times in the rest of the New Testament.

human being is capable of justifying himself or herself before God. Second, he employs the adverb translated "freely," which comes from a root meaning gift. Third, he identifies the ground or source of justification as God's grace, by which Paul points to the kindness, mercy, and unmerited favor of God. As we shall see, in Romans 4:4, Paul contrasts grace with obligation, indicating thus that it is a freely determined act of God's mercy. Fourth, he calls the process God used as the means of His grace "redemption." This word refers to an act that frees a person who was previously bound; so it shows justification as something done for us when we were helpless (see Romans 5:6) by somebody else. And fifth, he points to Christ Jesus as the one in whose person all this was accomplished.

For Paul, the theology and semantics of grace were not nearly so important (or interesting!) as the story of its accomplishment and effects. So he moves right on. "God presented him as a sacrifice of atonement, through faith in his blood" (Romans 3:25). In a manner similar to Hebrews 9:11-28, although not nearly in such detail as in that passage, Paul pictures Jesus as playing more than one role in the drama of redemption. Paul's shorthand is sometimes difficult to decipher. (See 2 Peter 3:15, 16.) The word translated "sacrifice of atonement" is in other versions rendered "propitiation" or "expiation." It is the word used in the Septuagint (the Greek translation of the Old Testament) to refer to the mercy seat, or the covering, of the ark of the covenant in the Holy of Holies of the Jerusalem temple. This is where, on the day of atonement, the high priest took the blood from the sacrifice and offered it to God for the sins of the people. Thus, Paul portrays Jesus as both the sacrifice (in His blood) and the sign of God's presence and receptivity. The exact meaning of faith in this verse is unclear, since it could refer either to the faithfulness of Jesus in giving His life or the trust in His blood necessary for our reception of redemption. In any case, both are true and both emphases are clearly made by Paul in other verses.

There are three effects of this redemptive event mentioned in these last seven verses of the chapter. The importance for God is that it preserves His justice (Romans 3:25, 26). We need to be constantly reminded that *justice* and *righteousness* and *justification* are all translations of the very same Greek word. So for the Greek-speaking Christian, dealing with God's justice was more than considering this or that action; it meant considering the

42

divine nature—righteousness. God had decided to leave unpunished the sins committed before the death of Jesus and to justify the one who has faith in Jesus. In order to do this and at the same time to be righteous/just, God demonstrated His righteousness/justice by means of the death of Jesus. Paul puts the same proclamation in other terms in 2 Corinthians 5:18-21:

> All this is from God, who reconciled us to himself through Christ and gave us the ministry of reconciliation: that God was reconciling the world to himself in Christ, not counting men's sins against them. And he has committed to us the message of reconciliation.
>
> We are therefore Christ's ambassadors, as though God were making his appeal through us. We implore you on Christ's behalf: Be reconciled to God. God made him who had no sin to be sin for us, so that in him we might become the righteousness of God.

The full implications of such a divine necessity are beyond human understanding. But we can appreciate how far our gracious God was willing to go to make possible the redemption of His rebellious creatures.

The effect that such an act of redemption should have on the man or woman who receives it is the exclusion of boasting or of any feeling of pride (Romans 3:27-30). The only good reason a human being could have for pride is some human accomplishment. Paul has made it clear that the accomplishment of redemption is all God's. The only part we play in the process is what Paul refers to here as faith. We have already seen that the term faith carries more significance than mere intellectual assent. It involves also trust and loyalty. But all of these are responses to God's initiative. Faith is vital to the process, and faith is a matter of choice, as we shall see in the next chapter. But faith is no grounds for glorying, since it shows neither individual initiative (it is a response to God's initiative) nor special ability (it is a possibility for Jew and Gentile alike).

Finally, the effect of justification by faith must be felt in our understanding of God's law. It does not "nullify the law.... Rather, we uphold the law" (Romans 3:31). Paul just leaves this affirmation here. He will deal with it more fully in chapters 4—7.

Once again, we see how seriously God takes sin. Not only should we be impressed with the wickedness of sin, but we are also led to consider how far God was willing to go to deal with sin.

When we see sin as a master holding us as slaves in bondage, we should see God as willing to pay the price for our freedom. In 1 Corinthians, where Paul writes so much about the cross of Christ, he writes twice (6:20 and 7:23), "You were bought at a price." And what a price! The very life of the only-begotten Son of God flowed out in His blood for your sins and mine. The cross is the clearest statement imaginable of how seriously God takes sin.

The cross states loud and clear the fact that forgiveness is not easy, even for God. It informs us that God never intended that His human creatures should sin and, therefore, require forgiveness. He would rather not have to forgive sins. But to solve the problem of human sin, God got into the forgiveness business, which is a risky business, a painful business. "God made him who had no sin to be sin for us, so that in him we might become the righteousness of God" (2 Corinthians 5:21). An instrument of torture and death cannot symbolize easy forgiveness or cheap grace.

In Tennyson's dramatic poem, *Idylls of the King,* the poet shows how sensitive he was to the pain of God's forgiveness by putting the expression of it in the mouth of King Arthur. He is confronting Queen Guinevere after her infidelity. She has prostrated herself before him, and along with his expressions of pain and wrath, she hears these words:

> 'Yet think not that I come to urge thy crimes,
> I did not come to curse thee, Guinevere,
> I, whose vast pity almost makes me die
> To see thee, laying there thy golden head,
> My pride in happier summers, at my feet.
> The wrath which forc'd my thoughts on that fierce law,
> The doom of treason and the flaming death
> (When I first learnt thee hidden here), is past.
> The pang—which while I weigh'd thy heart with one
> Too wholly true to dream untruth in thee,
> Made my tears burn—is also past—in part.
> And all is past, the sin is sinn'd, and I,
> Lo! I forgive thee, as Eternal God
> Forgives![17]

---

[17]"Guinevere," lines 529ff.

The eternal God abhors sin, so that His wrath must be revealed against it; but He loves His human creatures, so that His grace is revealed to save us from His wrath. The cross, the symbol of the God-abandoned Son of God, shows how seriously God takes us and our sin. Thus, Paul and the other first-century Christian leaders reacted with shock to any hint of an attempt to permit the coexistence of sin and salvation. They recognized the continuing power of temptation but urged the rejection of sin by pointing out the absurdity and inappropriateness of continuing in sin. The most dangerous temptation of all for the believer appears to be the tendency to take lightly that which was the cause of the death of Christ. The cross demands that we take sin as seriously as God does.

Lord, Lord —
Why have you forsaken me?

"The cross demands that we take sin as seriously as God does."

CHAPTER FOUR

The Reception of the Gospel

Romans 4:1-25

Romans 4 is one of the finest examples in the New Testament of Jewish exposition of the Bible. In the form called "midrash," commonly used by first-century rabbis to teach in the synagogues, Paul here makes his point about the nature and function of faith. He has already made the point that the willful sin of each of us human beings has severed us from our Creator and that God opened a way back through the death and resurrection of Jesus. Now Paul must show how we can enter that way. The apostle was obviously aware that this is the point where the gospel as he preached it differed most radically from Judaism, including most Jewish understandings of Christianity. The Jews were not without their doctrine of grace.[18] But they generally considered it impossible for a person to enter that covenant of grace without somehow demonstrating his or her righteousness.

Paul, on the other hand, argues that all that is either possible or necessary on the part of the sinner is faith. As we have already noted, his conception of faith is not limited to an intellectual assent to some proposition, but is rather a personal commitment to Jesus as Lord, which implies acts of obedience. We can summarize the opposing positions thus: the Jewish-legalist Christian insists that a person is justified by means of certain acts of righteousness, while Paul argues that one is justified by the commitment of faith in Christ and is then enabled to do works of righteousness.

In order to argue this point with his fellow Jewish Christians, Paul sees it important to use a major Jewish teaching form. Thus,

---

[18]This is shown clearly in E. P. Sanders, *Paul and Palestinian Judaism* (Philadelphia: Fortress Press, 1977), pp. 33-430.

this midrash. Verse 1 clearly connects the chapter with the few verses preceding it, in which Paul insisted that observing the law is not a means of justification, but that faith is. The obvious place for one to go for answers to such a dilemma is the Jewish Bible, and the natural starting point is Abraham, the father of the nation and the first one with whom the Lord made a universal covenant and to whom the Lord gave circumcision as a sign of that covenant.

The Jewish midrash form used two texts: the main text was usually from the Torah (Genesis through Deuteronomy) and the auxiliary text from the Prophets or Psalms. In this case, the texts had to deal with justification. So Paul chose the Torah text, Genesis 15:6, and the other from Psalm 32. He sets up the argument in verse 2 with a reference to Romans 3:27 (boasting is excluded if faith is our only access to justification) and to Abraham (if he was justified by works, he had something to boast about). Then (in Romans 4:3) he quotes the text, "Abraham believed God, and it was credited to him as righteousness."

Paul's first expository step here is linguistic. He carefully analyzes the use of words in the text, emphasizing the word *credited* as a contrast to work and the obligation of wages. Therefore, he argues, Abraham's faith cannot be considered a work of righteousness. Rather (here he says something scandalous in a legalistic frame of reference), faith is commitment to the "God who justifies the wicked" (Romans 4:5).

At this point, he offers Psalm 32:1 and 2 as an additional warrant for his argument that faith is not a legalistic work. The linguistic link between the two texts is the word translated "count against him" (Romans 4:8). In the Greek, it is the same root word as translated "credited" in verse 3. And in this Psalm, three parallel statements are made about sin, using the terms *forgiven, covered,* and *never count against him.* So he is obviously dealing here not with a peripheral matter, but with the very heart of the gospel—the forgiveness of sins. This, of course, is the major blessing of God to humankind.

"Is this blessedness only for the circumcised, or also for the uncircumcised?" This question, which opens verse 9, leads into Paul's most convincing argument. Here he leaves linguistics and employs historical analysis. In verses 2-8, he has argued that Abraham was justified "apart from law." But, one might object, Abraham was circumcised; is that not a work of the law? Here the simple question is asked, "Was it [his justification] after he was circumcised, or before?" (Romans 4:10). A look at the early portion of the Genesis story of Abraham (chapters 15—17) reveals the answer. The record of his circumcision appears in Genesis 17:10, which records events several years removed from those recorded in Genesis 15:1-6. So Paul can conclude that Abraham "received the sign of circumcision, a seal of the righteousness that he had by faith, while he was still uncircumcised" (Romans 4:11). This simple historical fact should have convinced anybody who understood circumcision as the paradigmatic work of the law that indeed "it was not through law that Abraham ... received the promise ... but through the righteousness that comes by faith" (Romans 4:13).[19]

Paul's conclusion is stated in verses 11 and 12, and reiterated in verse 16: Abraham is "the father of us all." Since he was technically a Gentile (uncircumcised) when he was declared righteous, Abraham is the father of all uncircumcised believers. But this faith paternity applies also to the circumcised believers. Faith, in other words, is what connects us to God, to one another, and to Abraham; circumcision, or any other work of the law, does not determine those relationships. Righteous works, as Paul will show, are appropriate and important, but they are results and signs of our justification, not the means to it.

Romans 4:13-16 serves as a review/restatement, then, of the implications of Abraham's justification by faith. Here Paul also makes it clear that this experience was not peculiar to Abraham. This is the way God works His justification for us all. It is vital, therefore, that we understand just what faith is, just who its object is, and just how it works. To these concerns Paul turns in the rest of the chapter.

The nature of Abraham's faith is held up here as a model for ours. He believed in God (Romans 4:17); he believed in hope, against all hope (Romans 4:18), without weakening in his faith (Romans 4:19). He did not waver, but "was strengthened in his faith and gave glory to God, being fully persuaded that God had power to do what he had promised" (Romans 4:20, 21). That is an impressive picture of total commitment and trust. Romans 4:21

---

[19]Further discussion of Paul's use of the Old Testament will be deferred to our consideration of Romans 9—11.

seems to me to offer the closest thing we have in Romans to a definition of faith. As we might rephrase it, faith is taking God at His word. Faith is not an independent entity nor a source of power. It is, rather, the way for a person to relate to the Lord of the universe so that His power can flow. The defeat of weakness and wavering and the strengthening that comes with faith are a matter of God's doing what He promised. Faith is a human decision to trust the powerful God to fulfill His promises.

The key issue, then, is not how strong one's faith is, but who God is, as the object of one's faith. In this chapter, Paul has embedded three important statements about God. They appear in verses 5, 17, and 24, so that when one moves slowly through the chapter, he could easily miss the unity of the three. Actually, Paul composed them in parallel grammatical construction, which is indicated in English translations by the relative pronoun *who*. In each case, the "who" clause says something different about the God in whom we believe:

"God who justifies the wicked" (Romans 4:5).

"God who gives life to the dead and calls things that are not as though they were" (Romans 4:17).

"Him who raised Jesus our Lord from the dead" (Romans 4:24).

What is the connection between these three theological statements? The first and most obvious connection is that they are all about the same God. We should not discount the importance of this connection just because it is so obvious. The first statement, as we have already noted, would seem scandalous to people who maintain that the righteous God could have nothing to do with wicked persons. The third statement, as Paul discovered in Athens (Acts 17:32), seemed absurd to some. Of course, the second statement is hotly debated in our own age. Yet Paul insists that the God who justifies is not just a judge, but also the Creator and the One who raised Jesus from the dead.

The second connection between Paul's three theological statements is seen in the immediate context of the chapter. They all refer to the object of faith. In other words, they describe the God who is the object of true Christian faith. Paul is not so much interested in dealing philosophically with the nature of the

Divinity as he is concerned to describe God as He chooses to relate to humankind. Creation, justification, and even resurrection, as interesting as they may seem as subjects for reflection and discussion, are in Paul's eyes to be understood as acts of God for us.

A third connection takes this application even further, as we see in the larger context of the whole epistle. This faith Paul is discussing is but the means of our access to God's salvation or justification. The combination of these connections indicates that, in order to understand our salvation, we should understand something of the God who is its source and who is the object of the faith that makes it accessible to us.

Let's look again. In verse 5, Paul calls God the one who justifies. The terms *justify* and *justification* are forensic terms; that is, they are usually connected with a court of justice. In most instances of our age, a jury decides whether a defendant is guilty or not, but in Paul's age, such decisions were usually made by a single judge. The act of justification consisted of a judge's declaring the accused not guilty (just). So Paul here pictures God as the divine judge who declares that the wicked (guilty) person is just (not guilty). How could He do this? In Romans 3:21-26, Paul has already shown that the blood of Christ has made it possible for God to maintain His own justice (righteousness) while at the same time justifying the one who believes in Jesus. So in this first statement, God is described as the one who has presented Jesus as a substitute for us, taking the punishment for which we were liable, so that He could declare us righteous.

In Romans 4:17, Paul describes God in two different ways as the Creator. He "gives life to the dead and calls things that are not as though they were." These closing words could also be translated "calls things not being as being." For Paul, as for anybody trained in the Hebrew Scriptures, the call of God is powerful. God's call accomplishes the thing it speaks. He spoke the universe into being (Genesis 1 and 2 Corinthians 4:6) and called His people out of Egypt (Hosea 11:1). For Abraham's specific faith connection, God's ability to give life to the dead was the primary point, because what God was asking him to believe was that the ninety-nine-year-old Abraham and his almost-equally-aged wife would have a baby (Genesis 18:1-15).

In Romans 4:24, Paul makes the point that it was God who raised Jesus from the dead. The connection between this and verse

17 should be obvious. And Paul, in verse 25, makes the connection with verse 5, as he capsulizes the content of saving faith: "He was delivered over to death for our sins and was raised to life for our justification."

The resurrection is the link of this theology with the Christian gospel. The concern for justification is the major focus of Romans in regard to what we call salvation. And the talk about creation, as the central aspect of Abraham's faith, is the key theological idea in the chapter. How do we put it all together? Let's keep in mind the obvious connection—it is the same God who had power to call the universe into existence. He is the God who gave life to Abraham and Sarah. He is the God who showed His continuing power by raising Jesus from the dead. And He is the God who, as Judge, says to us sinners, "You are righteous." God's call of justification is seen by Paul as equivalent to His call of creation. This means that for Paul, salvation means new creation. He makes this clear not only in Romans 4 but also in 2 Corinthians 4:6—5:2 and in Galatians. The latter epistle has as one of its closing statements, "What counts is a new creation" (Galatians 6:15). Paul has not dealt with creation explicitly anywhere else in Galatians. What he has dealt with quite thoroughly (even using Abraham as a model in Galatians 3:6-9) is justification by grace through faith. This would indicate that Paul saw it as a general rule that when God forgives a person's sins for Christ's sake, He accomplishes something in that person's life. God's is not blind justice. He knows what sin is and takes it very seriously. But when God the Creator/Judge declares a person righteous, righteousness happens where there was none before. As he puts it in 2 Corinthians 5:21, "God made him who had no sin to be sin for us, so that in him we might become the righteousness of God."

Christians in every age need to recognize the force of that word *become.* The process of justification is not confined to the mind of God. Too often we depict God as the Judge saying to the sinner, "I know you are a sinner, and you know you are a sinner, but I'll treat you as if you were righteous." One hears, in fact, people defining justification as God's treating us sinners "just as if" we were innocent. But the New Testament witnesses are unanimous in proclaiming that something radical has happened. In Christ's death and resurrection, the situation of justice in the whole creation has been altered, and in the act of justification, God remakes the sinner so that this formerly wicked person "becomes" not only righteous but, even more, "the righteousness of God."

For this reason, the writers of the New Testament documents use the most radical terms available to discuss what we call salvation. John (3:3-8) quotes Jesus discussing the new birth—a birth from above. His reference to being born of water and spirit would certainly have caused a Jewish leader like Nicodemus to think about Genesis 1:2, where we are told that "the Spirit of God was hovering over the waters." So Paul's terminology of new creation is consistent with the teaching of Jesus himself. Both Paul and John return repeatedly to such radical thinking in their use of contrasts in reference to salvation. The Christian is one who has been transported from darkness to light (John 8:12; 12:35-46; 1 John 1:5, 6; 2:8, 9; 2 Corinthians 6:14; Ephesians 5:8-11; Colossians 1:13; 1 Thessalonians 5:4, 5; cf. 1 Peter 2:9), from death to life (John 5:21-30; 1 John 3:14; Romans 5:12-21; 6:3-13; 2 Corinthians 2:16; 2 Timothy 1:10; cf. James 5:20). We have been changed from slaves to free persons (John 8:32-36; Romans 6:15-23; 2 Corinthians 3:17; Galatians 5:1), from enemies of God to His own children (Romans 5:10; 8:16-21; Galatians 4:5; John 1:12; 1 John 3:1-10; cf. 1 Peter 1:14).

Faith, then, is not wishful thinking or self-hypnosis. Faith is the means by which we allow God to proceed with His radical reconstruction of our lives. Unless we see that the nature and structure of life as the world knows it is in the process of transformation by the Creator himself, we miss the point of grace, faith, justification, and the very act of redemption in Christ, which is the heart of the Christian message. In addition to this, our failure to grasp the full import of new creation surely leaves us with the kinds of inferiority complexes that paralyze us and our congregations with fear in the face of a threatening world. Christians who order their lives as though nothing really changed with their obedience of faith are destined for repeated failure. But those who begin to live as walking "in the newness of life" (Romans 6:4, KJV) will be able to say, "I can do everything through him who gives me strength" (Philippians 4:13). All this is made possible by and implied in the proclamation that "he was delivered over to death for our sins and was raised to life for our justification" (Romans 4:25).

CHAPTER FIVE

The Effects of the Gospel

Romans 5:1-11

Here we arrive at a new phase of the development of Paul's thought. Whereas in Romans 1:16—4:25, Paul has dealt accusingly (note the use of the second person pronouns in Romans 2:1-21), most of that section argued his understanding of sin and justification in rather general and abstract terms. Even the major term, *justification/righteousness,* is a forensic abstraction. But Romans 5:1-11 shifts the emphasis closer to life as we live it. In fact, the pronouns *we* and *us* dominate this passage. Here, Paul begins to discuss justification in terms of peace with God and reconciliation. He writes about faith in terms of hope and love. He explains the grace of God in terms of Christ's death for sinners. In short, as C. E. B. Cranfield suggests, whereas in Romans 1:18—4:25, Paul has expounded the clause from Habakkuk 2:4, "He who is righteous by faith," now he turns to the rest of the sentence, "shall live."[20]

These eleven verses function, then, as a transition statement. The opening words summarize the substance of the former part of the letter. The rest begins to bring the whole discussion to the level of real life, where justification by grace through faith must be dealt with in terms of peace, obedience, freedom, internal tension, life in the domain of the Spirit, and the effect of all this on the physical creation. This is precisely the outline of chapters 5—8. To fulfill such a transitional function, Paul introduces a whole new (to this epistle) glossary. Therefore, much of our study of these eleven verses will focus on word meanings.

---

[20]C. E. B. Cranfield, *Romans: A Shorter Commentary* (Grand Rapids: William B. Eerdmans Publishing Company, 1985), pp. 98f.

The first verse summarizes, as we have noted, Paul's proclamation that we (otherwise unrighteous, rebellious creatures) have been declared (and thereby created) righteous on the basis of faith. It then makes the further declaration that "we have peace with God through our Lord Jesus Christ." A number of ancient manuscripts state this as an exhortation, "Let us have peace. . . ." But most scholars understand that reading as a simple error by scribes in the early copying process, since the difference is just that the rejected form has a long *o* (Greek omega) where the accepted text has a short *o* (omicron). A scribe taking dictation could hardly have distinguished between the two sounds in the middle of a word. This is a good example of how a number of variant readings have crept into the Biblical text during the centuries before the invention of mechanical printing. It can well be called miraculous that we have such a trustworthy text of documents so ancient as are the books of our New and Old Testaments.

Peace is the new term in this verse. As we noted in reference to Romans 1:7, "peace" is the common translation of the Hebrew word *shalom*. For the Jewish Christian, *peace* meant much more than the absence of conflict. Paul makes clear here that it is first of all a restored relationship with God. Paul's theology is never simple. We saw in the last chapter how he links God as Judge with God as Creator. Here in chapter 5, he turns to very personal terms like *love, reconciliation,* and *peace with God.* We should guard against the tendency to conceive of God as a concept or an abstraction. The whole Bible insists that even though God is spirit and holy, He is also personal. In philosophical terms, God is simultaneously transcendent and imminent. He is "God, and not man," but He is also "the Holy One among you" (Hosea 11:9). Through our Lord Jesus Christ, we see most clearly God's refusal to be confined in an idea or a ritual or even a book. His ultimate self-revelation is as a person. Since this is so, God's act of justification of us sinners had to result in a restoration of the personal relationship for which He created humankind in the first place. The peace in which Adam walked and talked with God (Genesis 2:8-25) was turned to fear by sin (Genesis 3:8-10), but it has now been restored "through our Lord Jesus Christ."

Of course, *peace* was not exclusively a Jewish term. The Romans boasted of the *pax Romana.* This peace, guaranteed by the emperor and maintained by his troops, created an aura of security and stability within the Roman empire. People could live free of fears about foreign invasion, pirates, and robbers. Yet all fear was not removed. First-century Roman and Greek literature displays life-molding fears of the power of the stars, of demons, of the fates, of capricious deities, and of the even more present natural catastrophes. So for Jew and Greek alike, peace with the God who justifies the wicked was good news indeed.

The closing phrase of verse 1 is so familiar that we can easily overlook it. But Paul uses the Christian confession that all this happens "through our Lord Jesus Christ" four more times in chapters 5—8 in nearly the same form. Each of the four later appearances completes another step in his exposition (Romans 5:21; 6:23; 7:25; and 8:39). Thus, Paul unifies these four chapters as he explains what it means to "have peace with God through our Lord Jesus Christ."

The second verse offers two more results of our justification. The first of these is access to grace. The word translated "access" is also a personal word. It was used in reference to somehow winning an audience with a king or other high official. One usually did that through a friend in court. So Paul pictures Christ as our advocate—the one on the basis of whose recommendation we have "gained access ... into this grace in which we now stand." One hears often enough about "the state of grace" and about the question of whether or not a Christian can fall from grace. This second issue must be faced as we get to chapter 9, but here Paul does not picture grace so much as a position, but rather as an environment in which we live and from which we receive the necessities of the Christian life. *Grace,* in the vocabulary of the apostle, describes the unmerited mercy of God, which offers the sinner salvation, the further extension of that mercy, which makes it possible for the redeemed to serve God (Romans 1:5; cf. Ephesians 3:2-9), and the ongoing blessings of Christ, which Paul wishes to all in his benedictions (cf. 1 Corinthians 16:23; 2 Corinthians 13:14; Galatians 6:18). Here, in Romans 5:2, *grace* is that nourishing environment in which the Christian stands firm in the security to experience the next result of justification.

That second result is stated in the last sentence in the verse: "And we rejoice in the hope of the glory of God." *Rejoice* appears as a sort of theme word here, but it is really not new. In noun form, it has been used rather negatively and translated "boasting" in Romans 3:27 and 4:2. At Romans 5:2, however, it is clear that our status before God is not because of our merits, but because of God's grace. We receive His peace by faith, and we may therefore rejoice in our present, which is but a foretaste of God's glory to be experienced in the future. So the primary new idea here is hope. Paul mentioned hope in passing as he described Abraham's faith in Romans 4:18. Here it becomes a present reality for "all Abraham's offspring" (Romans 4:16), and Paul will return to it in chapter 8. That which we hope for is the glory of God. As we have indicated with reference to Romans 3:23, the glory of God for Paul and other Jewish students of the fall of humankind was lost as a result of sin and would be restored in the end time. Here is Paul's statement of that ultimate hope. The presence of God will certainly be glorious, as we customarily use the term, but it will also mean the restoration of fallen human beings to their originally intended nature. "All have sinned and lack the glory of God," but we sinners justified and living in grace and peace through Christ rejoice in the expectation of the restoration of our lost glory. (Note the progression Romans 3:23; 3:24; 4:5; 4:25; 5:2; 5:5.)

In Romans 5:3, Paul highlights what appears, from a worldly point of view, to be the opposite of rejoicing in hope of glory. "Not only so," he writes, "but we also rejoice in our sufferings." To suffer purposefully in order to bring the flesh under control and thus free the spirit was a practice taught and used by the Stoic philosophers. To suffer pain for the glory of Rome was a mark of honor for the Roman legionnaire. Suffering was likewise tolerated by the pious Jew as a sign of God's discipline. But to glory in it, to boast about it, to exult or rejoice in it would have seemed more than a bit strange then. In twentieth-century western cultures, where for most people real suffering can be avoided, it seems sick to speak of rejoicing in suffering. But the early Christians had been confronted with an event that had completely changed their point of view. They had seen, either with their own eyes or by means of the proclamation of the gospel, Christ crucified. (See Galatians 3:1.) They saw that to confess the crucified Jesus as living Lord and Christ meant that they had entered a mode of being in which suffering was a necessary means of redeeming a fallen creation. Their general attitude seems to have been, "Since Christ suffered for me, my suffering participates somehow in the same process of redemption." (See Colossians 1:24 and 1 Peter 1:6-9.)

It seems obvious that only with such a total change of mind (repentance) could the following series of claims be accepted as true. "We know that suffering produces perseverance" (Romans 5:3). This last word, which is translated in earlier versions "patience," is descriptive of active strength—the disciplined patience of the long-distance runner. So *perseverance* is the better choice. Paul observed such perseverance resulting from suffering, and he was confident that other Christians did, too. But we do not always see that happening. As many of this world's goods as most of us possess, we still know the shock of seeing a daughter bleeding in a hospital emergency room or the ache of watching a disease sap the strength of a young man or the depression that sets in while one learns to cope with a relative or friend with a mental handicap or illness. Most of us have also seen such experiences ruin the stability of those involved and tear families apart. Paul is not generalizing here. Suffering does not always produce endurance. That happens only in the suffering of those of us who hope for the glory of God and, thus, are not in a position to be overwhelmed by the events and conditions of this life.

Verse 4 continues, "Perseverance, character." Given the kind of hopeful faith that causes suffering to produce perseverance, such endurance will show itself in what we call character. The Greek word here indicates something tested and proved. It appears again in Romans 12:2, where it is translated, "Then you will be able to test and approve what God's will is." The believer who perseveres through suffering will be marked with a recognizable stamp of approval—solid character.

Such character, then, brings us back to "hope." This might sound as though we are going around in circles, but it is more like a spiral. *Hope* here stands by itself. Paul mentions no specific object, as he does in verse 2. Here, hope seems to be a total mindset. He is not pushing blind optimism, but the attitude that develops through the continuing experience of peace with God in all circumstances—the trust that says not only, "He did," but also, "He will." This is not wishful thinking, but rather faith-grounded, experience-developed optimism.

Verse 5, then, brings us back to the divine initiative that makes all our human growth possible. Paul's words here echo Psalm 22:5, "They cried to you and were saved; in you they trusted and were not disappointed." Paul exults, "And hope does not disappoint us, because God has poured out his love into our hearts by the Holy Spirit, whom he has given us." In the clause following *because,* the NIV translators have solved a problem for us. The Greek reads literally, "The love of God is poured out...." Most commentaries trace the age-old argument about whether Paul meant God's love for us or our love for God. Such arguments stem from the penchant of scholars to try to explain just how God does everything. But Paul is not concerned here to explain how faith, hope, or love come about. He is trying, in rather poetic fashion, to picture God's abundant mercy and generosity. In verse 8, he makes it clear that he is thinking about God's love for us, which He poured out into our hearts. The Bible speaks also of God's wrath being poured out (Psalm 69:24) and also His Spirit (Joel 3:1, 2; Acts 2:17; Titus 3:5, 6). Jesus used the same word to explain the fruit of the vine as His blood "poured out" (Mark 14:24 and parallels). With no attempt to explain the mechanics of it, but in concert with other early Christian writers, Paul points to the fact of God's abundant gift of His love, which comes to us by means of another (unexplained and perhaps unexplainable) gift, God's Holy Spirit. A fuller discussion of the Holy Spirit must be reserved for chapter 8. It will suffice now just to call attention to the fact that everything we have as Christians comes as a gift. We need to respond in order to receive the gift, but the initiative is God's, and we can claim neither right nor worth in the transaction. It is, then, certainly a cause for rejoicing.

In Romans 5:6-8, Paul shows how Christ's death reveals the extent of God's love. In verse 6, he uses two adjectives to show that the timing of Christ's death was providential. Only the merciful God would choose the time when we (note how personal He is here) were still "powerless" and "ungodly." The word translated "ungodly" is the first word Paul had employed to describe the willful, rebellious sinners in Romans 1. (See verse 18.) This is clearly a mess we got ourselves into, but once in it, we were helpless. Paul will soon examine sin as an enslaving force; so he is not using empty rhetoric here. It is for the helpless and ungodly that Christ died.

Contrast that, he suggests, with our human attitudes. "Very rarely will anyone die for a righteous man." We should note that "man" does not appear in Paul's text. He does not so limit this statement, but his point is clear: although selfless sacrifice happens, it is rare. "Though for a good man someone might possibly dare to die." The term translated "good man" could refer to a personal benefactor and thus carry overtones of obligation. But in any case, Paul's point is the extreme contrast between our hesitance to die for even good people and God's willingness to die for the ungodly. So in verse 8, he states the point clearly. The second half of the verse parallels verse 6, substituting *sinners* for *ungodly*. The first half makes Paul's theological point of the extent of God's love for us.

Verses 9 and 10 introduce two more terms for our consideration of the results of justification: *salvation* and *reconciliation*. We should, in passing, note that the opening clause of verse 9 makes it clear that Paul does not try to distinguish between the results of Christ's death and those of His resurrection, as Romans 4:25 could cause us to think. Here, Christ's blood is the cause of our justification, just as, in Romans 4:25, His resurrection is. The crucifixion and resurrection of Christ are, for Paul, a single event by which God made possible the justification of the ungodly. If such justification is a present reality, then "how much more shall we be saved from God's wrath through him!" The phrase *how much more* appears often in Paul's arguments. He uses it three more times in this chapter alone. It is the sign of a well-known and accepted Jewish rhetorical principle with which, when one point is made, it goes nearly without saying that a parallel (but perhaps less difficult) point is also true. Paul has already used the noun form of *salvation* in Romans 1:16, just before he dealt with God's wrath. Now that he has established that forgiveness has come through Christ, he can assure us that we need fear the wrath no longer. When the day of wrath comes, we are assured salvation from it. Since the word *salvation* has medical overtones, perhaps we can deal with it here in terms of preventive medicine. As long as we are right with Christ, we are immune to the destructive power of God's wrath.

In Romans 5:10, Paul turns to the domain of personal relationships to complete the picture of the results of justification. "When we were God's enemies, we were reconciled to him through the death of his Son." The parallelism with verses 6 and 8 shows that being ungodly and sinners means being enemies of God. Since sin was the cause of this enmity, Christ's being "delivered over to death for our sins and [being] raised to life for our justification" (Romans 4:25) does away with the cause of the enmity and, thus, accomplishes reconciliation. The extent of this restored relationship is discussed in Romans 8:12-17. For now,

Paul is content to use the fact of it as another warrant for his point: "How much more, having been reconciled, shall we be saved through his life!"

In Romans 5:11, Paul brings us back to his starting point in verse 2—our rejoicing in the new relationship with God. Even though verse 11 does not introduce anything new to the discussion, it should remind us of the Christian's natural reaction of rejoicing. To express joy for freedom, for a renewed relationship, and for a glorious hope for the future is a quite natural tendency. In fact, if something that important happened to somebody, we would consider it very strange if that person did not somehow express joy. For the Christian, worship (rejoicing in the Lord; Ephesians 4:4-7) should be a natural celebration of the good news. The statements of joy, praise, and thanksgiving that punctuate the New Testament are not typical elements of first-century culture. They are natural results of God's gracious act of justification. Worship as our response to the gospel should be our continuing experience also.

CHAPTER SIX

The Superiority of the Gospel
Romans 5:12-21

It could be argued that Romans 5:12-21 has been the basis for more prolonged controversy in Christian doctrine than any other single passage of the Bible. Beginning in the fourth century, Romans 5:12 became the keystone of the doctrine of original sin. Augustine and his followers taught that in Adam's sin, every person to be born already sinned, so that each person is born a sinner. Such a doctrine of mass perdition and total depravity was undergirded by Jerome's translation of this verse into the Latin in the version called the Vulgate. He rendered the two little words in the Greek text that mean "for that" or "because" with the Latin *in quo* ("in whom"), so that it appears that the apostle explains death's coming to all because all sinned in Adam. Linked with a strained understanding of Romans 5:5, that the pouring out of God's love is actually an infusion of grace to make it possible for a person to believe, this doctrine of sin and salvation dominated Christian theology for over a thousand years and undergirded both the Roman Catholic sacramental system and the Calvinistic doctrine of total depravity. It is only recently that Calvinist, Catholic, and other scholars have begun to recognize that this passage should not be used to support such thinking, since neither Paul's background nor his obvious intent would take him in that direction.

What is he trying to do by bringing Adam and Christ together in the way he does? Our examination of the passage must look carefully at what he argues and what he does not argue on the basis of this Adam-Christ comparison. For this purpose, we need to observe the context of the passage. At first glance, this section seems to interrupt, or at least detour, the line of thought somewhat. In Romans 5:11, we "rejoice in God through our Lord Jesus Christ." In Romans 5:12, Paul begins a discussion of how sin entered the world. The connecting phrase, which is translated "therefore," is so indefinite as to point to no explicit antecedent nor to any special relationship. As we have seen, verses 1-11 summarize what precedes and introduce themes that Paul develops more fully through chapter 8 to describe the results of justification on the basis of faith. It appears, then, that verses 1-11 form an introduction to a new section of the epistle and that verses 12-21 comprise the first step into that section. Paul wants to deal with sin (chapters 5 and 7) and redemption (6 and 8) in relation to the law (Romans 5:13—8:4), and so he decides to begin at the beginning, as he did in a less concrete way in Romans 1:18. We should keep in mind the discussion of sin in Romans 1:18—3:20 as we proceed to finish chapter 5 and later examine chapter 7.

In addition, we should note that Paul's Jewish tradition offered him a ready-made backdrop for this discussion. We can expect that Genesis 3 would be in the apostle's mind in any treatment of Adam and sin, and we can sense that it is there, although it becomes more explicit in chapter 7. For chapter 5, the more direct connection is with the Jewish teaching about Adam. In addition to the references mentioned in our discussion of Romans 3:23, several other Jewish documents hold that all of humankind fell into sin through Adam's (or Eve's) fall and that death resulted.[21] They maintain that position while at the same time insisting that each individual is responsible for his or her own sin.

Thus, Paul had a framework of Adam speculation in which to work out his Adam-Christ typology. He did not follow the more fantastic speculative lines, but he dealt with Adam as the first man and first sinner, whose nature and inclinations all persons share.

In addition to looking at the context in Judaism and in the epistle, we are forced by Paul's writing style to analyze the structure of this passage. To read through it quickly could be confusing; but if we recognize that Paul begins his statement in verse 12 and then interrupts himself with a series of contrasts in verses 13-17, we can pick up his train of thought in verse 18 and then fit the whole statement together.

---

[21]Sirach 25:24; 2 Esdras 3:21f and 4:30; 4 Ezra 3:7 and 7:116-126; Life of Adam and Eve 28; and 2 Baruch 17:3 and 19:8.

So then, keeping in mind that the apostle's intent is to contrast the results of Adam's disobedience (sin, condemnation, and death) and those of Christ's obedience (righteousness, salvation, and life), we enter the stream of his thinking at verse 12. Here, Paul introduces several revealing thoughts. He makes it clear that sin was not a part of God's original creation. "Sin entered the world through one man, and death through sin." Ignoring for the time being any talk about fallen angels, a serpent, Eve, or evil impulses, he portrays sin's entrance into the cosmos simply as an act of an individual. But on the other hand, the sin that thus entered is presented as more than an isolated act—also more than a long series of acts. It is a power that stands here and in chapters 7 and 8 against the power and authority of the Creator. In fact, it contradicts the intent of the Creator, since He is the giver of life, and sin ushered in the reality and reign of death. (See Romans 4:17.)

The second part of the verse is more problematic: "And in this way death came to all men, because all sinned." The first problem is, of course, the relationship of sin and death or that of sin and suffering. It is too easy to conclude that suffering or death is a direct result of sin. The story of Job should warn us not to be too quick to judge individuals on the basis of the circumstances of their lives. This is precisely what Jesus' disciples got caught up in, according to John 9:1-3, when they saw a blind man and asked Jesus, "Who sinned, this man or his parents, that he was born blind?" Jesus' reply was, "Neither this man nor his parents sinned, but this happened so that the work of God might be displayed in his life."

How can we reconcile that with what Paul says in Romans 5? We should, first of all, guard against the spiritualizing tendency that says *death* in Paul means only eternal separation from God. That is to import a foreign world view into Paul's thought. He could not so easily distinguish between physical death and spiritual death. His view of human nature is unitive; that is, he sees the person as a unit. Therefore, when he writes *death,* he refers to total death—both physical and spiritual. A corollary to that is his understanding of eternal life—not in the Greek sense of the immortality of the soul, but in the Christian sense of a miraculous, total resurrection.

Second, we should note that Paul's statement is quite general. We could paraphrase it, "Through one person, sin entered the cosmic picture and through sin death, and thus death became a reality for all persons." We should not force Paul to say more here than simply that Adam's sin became the opening through which death entered human experience. Does this mean that the apostle saw death as an unnatural element in creation? It seems so. A close reading of Genesis 2 and 3 reveals that God did not deny Adam and Eve access to the tree of life until after they had disobeyed Him by eating of the tree of the knowledge of good and evil. Therefore, we should expect Paul to treat death as an interloper—as not being part of the Creator's original intent—which is just what we discover here.

The second problem here we have already alluded to: the relationship between Adam's sin and our responsibility. The final clause of verse 12 seems rather clear in this regard, "because all sinned." We cannot escape responsibility for what happens to us. Even though we dare not assume a direct correlation between specific transgressions and specific pains or problems, yet our own sins leave us liable and vulnerable to the general results of sin in the world. Specific events may seem unjust, but in a world dominated by sin (unrighteousness/injustice), we can hardly expect any better. Because we all sin, we stand open to the power of the destroyer—power that was granted entrance by Adam's sin, and can be overcome only by action of the Creator.

With verse 13 begins a digression. As we noted earlier, this digression lasts through verse 17. (The NIV marks the break with a dash.) The first question Paul must deal with in regard to sin and human history is the place of the law of Moses. It is clear that Adam disobeyed a direct command and that after the giving of the law on Mount Sinai, the Jews have had (and have disobeyed) direct commands. How should we understand the period between Adam and Moses? "For before the law was given, sin was in the world." It must have been, since people died. "But sin is not taken into account when there is no law." The reader might be disappointed that this commentary can offer no clear and unequivocal explanation of Paul's meaning in this latter statement. There seem to be two major viable options. The first is based on the verb translated "taken into account." In its only other appearance in the New Testament, Paul writes to Philemon (verse 18) about the runaway slave, Onesimus, "If he has done you any wrong or owes you anything, charge it to me." This closing phrase is where he uses the verb in question, which comes from the world of accounting. Literally, then, Romans 5:13b could be translated, "But sin is not registered on the books, there being no law." This would point to the conception of God's final judgment as the time when the books will be opened in which are registered the actions (good and bad) of each individual. This is similar to what Paul has already stated in Romans 2:5-11. The problem is, of course, that this would leave those who lived between Adam and Moses free of guilt on the day of judgment, which seems to contradict the context of Romans 1:18—2:24.

The second interpretation understands the verb as being used figuratively and reflectively. It is possible that Paul's use of the bookkeeping term here refers to human consciousness rather than God's judgment. In other words he could mean, "Without law one does not realize the gravity of sin." This is similar to what he will say in Romans 7:7-13. So we are left with a quandary. The second option seems to me to present fewer problems and to fit better with the way Paul's thought is developing, but it must be admitted that the first is the normal use of the terms. This could well be one example of what 2 Peter 3:16 refers to with the statement that Paul's letters "contain some things that are hard to understand."

At any rate, verse 14 reminds us that "death reigned from the time of Adam to the time of Moses, even over those who did not sin by breaking a command, as did Adam, who was a pattern of the one to come." Paul has already shown that even those who never had God's written revelation had, nevertheless, revelation that leaves them without excuse (Romans 1:18-23; 2:14, 15). So it cannot be considered unjust that they all suffered death, the result of sin. For some reason (perhaps to remind readers of the main theme of this passage), Paul closes verse 14 with the reference to Adam as (literally) a "type of the coming." Some have decided that "the one to come" must refer to Moses, since he is mentioned in the sentence. But there is no real comparison of Adam and Moses; so this seems unlikely. Others have insisted that "that which is coming" (it is not necessarily masculine) refers to all humanity as descended from Adam. This fits rather nicely into the use of the passage to prove inherited sin; but the fact that Paul uses a singular construction makes such an understanding questionable. It seems more likely that Paul is referring again, with a sort of shorthand, to the theme of the whole passage—the comparison/contrast of Adam and Christ. In fact, the use of the Greek word *typos* (pattern, type) here leads most commentators to describe what Paul does in Romans 5:12-21 as his Adam-Christ typology.

Romans 5:15-17 makes clear that Paul's typology is not what we call analogy. There is but one positive comparison between Adam and Christ. The other points are contrasts. The similarity between Adam and Christ consists basically in the fact that each did something that had cosmological results. Otherwise, Adam is seen in a negative light and Christ, totally positive. Adam disobeyed, which began a process in conflict with the original creation and, therefore, with the Creator. Christ obeyed, and thus began a new process of creation in harmony with the Creator. This new creation is repeatedly referred to here as God's gift of grace, which contrasts with death as a domineering result of Adam's sin. In verse 15, Paul shows that the gift is made available (overflowingly) to the same (many) people as are affected by the trespass and its resultant death. But he shows the contrast by overloading the Christ side of the statement. The NIV has twice as many words in the second half, and the original Greek has an even more lopsided ratio. Then, in verse 16, Paul shows a definite contrast: sin brought the judgment of condemnation (resulting from one sin), but the gift (following numerous trespasses) brought justification, a term that, by now, clearly carries great weight in Paul's understanding. Paul caps off this series in verse 17, both by the imbalance of his sentence and by contrasting the ultimate result of each side. The result of Adam's sin is that "death reigned." However, in contrast, "how much more will those who receive God's abundant provision of grace and of the gift of righteousness reign in life through the one man, Jesus Christ." This verse highlights both the contrast and the cosmological struggle. Both clauses center the action on the verb *reign,* the first time in the past tense, then in the future. The subject of the first is *death* and of the second is *those who receive*—that is, we Christians, who receive the abundance of grace and of the gift of righteousness. That which made possible the reign of death was one man's disobedience, while the enabler of the Christians' reign is Jesus Christ. The only phrase that has no parallel is *in life.* Death is definitely conceived of here as a power, in rather personal terms, but life is not an independent entity. Life is the gift of the Creator. This is made even clearer in verse 18, where "life for all" is the result of God's act of justification.

Verses 18 and 19 are finely crafted parallel statements. The two verses parallel each other, and each verse is composed of two parallel, although contrasting, statements. Furthermore, they both function as summaries of Paul's point in this section. In verse 18, the apostle contrasts the result of the "one trespass" ("condemnation") with that of the "one act of righteousness" ("justification that brings life for all"). Similarly, in verse 19, he contrasts the result of "the disobedience of the one man" ("many were made sinners") with that of "the obedience of the one man" ("many will be made righteous"). We should note especially three elements of these statements. First, we should recognize the importance of the contrast between Adam's disobedience and Christ's obedience. Adam disobeyed a direct command; so his act is accurately termed a trespass. But Christ lived and died in obedience to the full implication of God's grace (Hebrews 5:8—"Although he was a son, he learned obedience from what he suffered"), and so His sacrifice can be called an act of righteousness.

Second, therefore, what we have here is more than an example story. The Christian life is much more than a matter of choosing the right example to follow. Adam's trespass gave the powerful reality of sin and death entree to human life. And Christ's obedience makes righteousness, and thereby real life, a possibility for human beings. That brings us to the third element—the creation terminology in Romans 5:19. The verb Paul uses to note the result of the action of both Adam and Christ is a term that strongly expresses causation. The one caused or made the many to be sinners; the other, to be righteous. Sin and righteousness imply certain kinds of behavior patterns, but in this context, these statements go much farther than visible behavior. Paul is teaching here that sin, even though it was not part of God's intent for His creatures, has become such a normal part of human experience that he can say that "sin reigned" (Romans 5:12). On the other hand, righteousness is God's original intent, but the reign of sin has caused it to be abnormal until the only way we can attain it is to receive it as a gift. God through Christ has made us righteous and, thus, has overcome the grip of sin and death.

The last two verses of chapter 5 return to the role of the law in this drama of sin and grace. But the law is the focus of only one statement: "The law was added so that the trespass might increase" (Romans 5:20). It is hard to imagine Paul's claiming that God's purpose in giving the law was to cause people to sin more, although the wording of the sentence would permit that understanding. It is, rather, more likely that he has in mind that the fact of a commandment makes it clear just what sin is—disobedience or trespass. But the reality of the situation is the increase of sin in the world, whether because of, or in spite of, the law; and such increasing need called for a radical solution. So, "where sin increased, grace increased all the more." As Ulrich Wilckens points out, what the apostle describes in this statement and verse 21 is the negation of negation.[22] The Creator made everything, including humankind, to be very good (Genesis 1:31); sin negated this goodness; and grace has set it right again. Thus, God's event of redemption "through Jesus Christ our Lord" is the negation of negation. It is God's resounding YES to His creation. "So also grace might reign through righteousness to bring eternal life through Jesus Christ our Lord" (Romans 5:21).

We see Paul here proclaiming not only the negation of sin, but also explicitly the negation of death. If grace reigns in the Christian, then why do we continue to recoil from death? Before we whip ourselves too much over this, as though it must be considered a sign of lack of faith, let's be sure to understand the depth of what the apostle describes here. It is clear that he considers neither sin nor death as having been part of God's original creation. It is as though they were waiting in the wings during the drama of creation and made their entrance later through Adam and Eve. Death is not a natural phenomenon, as it was considered in Stoic philosophy and too often is for modern Stoics; but it is an incursion into God's creation. It is an enemy—the ultimate enemy, as Paul puts it in 1 Corinthians 15:26. It is, then, natural for us—and especially for us Christians—to find death distasteful, whether it is our own death or that of somebody else. Children of the Creator naturally have an aversion to the destroyer. Indeed, the human struggle between good and evil is really part of the cosmic struggle between life and death. This struggle is central, as Paul recognized, to the Christian faith, since the object of that faith is "the God who gives life to the dead" (Romans 4:17).

---

[22]*Der Brief an die Roemer* Vol. 1 (Zurich, Einsiedeln, Koeln: Benziger Verlag, 1978), pp. 330-337.

So this treatment of sin and death is more than a bare recital of facts or an explication of the nature of humankind. It describes the ultimate battle between God the Creator and Sin/Death the destroyer. It is understandable, therefore, that we have an aversion to death. But Paul gives us reason not to fear death nor to let it drive us to despair. The proclamation is about life, the winner. We recoil naturally from death, as Christ did at the grave of Lazarus (John 11:35, 38). But we need not fear it. In fact, we can welcome it because we believe the good news that Christ has triumphed over death, not only in some seemingly abstract, cosmic sense, but for our individual justification.

CHAPTER SEVEN

The Freedom Brought by the Gospel
Romans 6:1-23

With chapter 6, Paul carries his exposition of sin and salvation to another level by falling back on his diatribe style. In this style, he asks questions that, from a certain standpoint, would seem logical; and he replies to them with the logic demanded by the standpoint of the Christian faith. The chapter divides itself easily into two parts; verses 1-14 and verses 15-23. Each of these passages is an argument in itself, begun by a question. Each opening question (verses 1 and 15) connects with what went before. Each continues with a proposition in the form of a rhetorical question (verses 2 and 16). Each argument proceeds with an appeal to Christian experience (verses 2, 4 and 17, 18) and a reference to implications for life (verses 5-10 and 19b-22). Verses 11-14 return to the proposition in the form of an exhortation, which is followed by more exhortations. Verse 23 wraps up the whole argument with a promise in the form of a proposition.

Paul's opening question here causes the reader to wonder whether it could be considered an actual question or whether we should see it as the sort of rhetorical question that has an obvious negative reply. It seems to me that if we could follow his reasoning so far in the epistle without the advantage of what we know about the Christian faith and life, his question would seem rather sensible. "Shall we go on sinning so that grace may increase?" (Romans 6:1). Paul has finished chapter 5 with the claim that grace should rule in the place of sin. He has argued that grace is a gift of God and has nothing to do with the goodness or works of human beings. It seems reasonable that a person wanting to please God and coming to understand that God loves us so that He forgives us by grace would speculate about how best to please God. One option would be to allow Him to practice His grace by giving Him plenty of sins to forgive. The question about that is, of course

73

whether forgiveness is God's primary and favorite activity or whether it is secondary and practiced only because we make it necessary.

Paul sees easily through to the absurdity of the question, knowing that sin was not in the original intent of God, and thus, neither was forgiveness. So forgiveness should not be considered a primary activity of God; it is a secondary reaction to human need. Furthermore, "we died to sin; how can we live in it any longer?" (Romans 6:2). The grace of God works in such a way that it should not be necessary to have massive applications of it on a continuing basis. As we have already seen in Romans 4, God's work of justification by grace is a process of new creation. At this point, Paul brings death into the picture as a positive aspect of the new creation. In order to be newly created (or, in the terms of John 3, newly born), one must die to that which distinguishes the old life—sin. Paul claims that precisely this has happened in the experience of every Christian. Death to sin should change our point of view and our logic, and such a change makes Paul's opening question seem absurd.

Paul's positive use of death here shows clearly what we noted in the fifth chapter as the negation of negation. Christ's death and the Christian's death to sin sound both frightening and liberating—both negative and positive. When Paul says, "Or don't you know . . . ," he signals something every Christian should know—something Paul can assume is the experience and understanding of every believer. "All of us who were baptized into Christ Jesus were baptized into his death" (Romans 6:3). This indicates that Paul identified baptism as the event in which justification by grace through faith becomes a reality for the individual. J. S. Sweeney had good reason for preaching his sermon entitled, "Baptism For Remission of Sins Is Justification by Faith."[23]

Of course, Paul is not teaching baptism at this point. His intent is to guide Christians to a better understanding and application of their salvation to life. However, this realization makes this passage even more important for our understanding of baptism in the early church, since it shows us what was assumed to be practiced and understood by Christians everywhere. Paul had not founded

---

[23]This sermon is found in Z. T. Sweeney, ed., *New Testament Christianity* Vol. 1 (Columbus, IN: privately published, 1923), pp. 391-401.

the church at Rome; so he was not merely repeating his own teaching here. He assumed that they practiced and taught baptism in water as a burial of the old sinful humanity and a resurrection to new life in Christ. "We were therefore buried with him through baptism into death in order that, just as Christ was raised from the dead through the glory of the Father, we too may live a new life" (Romans 6:4). As C. E. B. Cranfield has written, "Baptism, according to Paul, while (as we have seen) it is no magical rite effecting mechanically that which it signifies, is no empty sign but a decisive event by which a particular [person] is powerfully and unequivocally claimed by God as a beneficiary of His saving deed in Christ."[24]

If Romans 5:20 left the impression that the quantity of grace is determined by the quantity of sin, Paul in Romans 6:1-14 wipes the impression out. The baptismal experience of the Christian, if taken seriously, should make it impossible for the Christian to entertain the notion of willfully sinning. Not only is that old sinful person dead, but a new person has replaced the old one. The new one lives with Christ. The Christian is not left to his or her own devices. The presence of Christ should mark out the life of the believer with power, in contrast to the powerlessness of sin, because of the crucifixion and resurrection (both His and ours). This means "we should no longer be slaves to sin—because anyone who has died has been freed from sin" (Romans 6:6, 7).

What Paul is describing here is what it means to be a Christian. The scholar might call it "Christian ontology." Paul's pattern is to discuss this first and then to turn to how a Christian should live. In this passage, the intent seems to be to teach Christian living by leading the believers to ponder what is appropriate behavior for the one who has been remade and is now living in the power of the resurrection. Our self-image includes not only who we are by natural birth, but also who we are by rebirth. In fact, for the Christian, the latter takes precedence. We have died to sin and been raised to life in Christ. This reflects the good news that Jesus died to sin and rose to life, with the result that "the death he died, he died to sin once for all; but the life he lives, he lives to God" (Romans 6:10). Since sin and death are in no way masters of

---

[24]C. E. B. Cranfield, *Romans: A Shorter Commentary* (Grand Rapids: William B. Eerdmans Publishing Co., 1985), p. 132.

Christ, and since the Christian is "united with him ... in his death" (Romans 6:5), it follows that sin and death, as powerful as they may seem, have no real power over the Christian. That power is ours to give or withhold as we will. If there is a single standard of Christian living, it is not law nor even the life of Jesus; it is His crucifixion and resurrection. The life of the follower of Jesus should reflect both the self-giving and the overcoming power that lie at the heart of the gospel.

Therefore, Paul can proceed to exhort his readers to consider themselves "dead to sin but alive to God in Christ Jesus," and not to "let sin reign in [their] mortal body so that [they] obey its evil desires" (Romans 6:11, 12). This return to the proposition stated in Romans 6:2 Paul expands with an appeal to the will of the believer. He seems not to be bothered by the apparent (but unreal?) conflict between salvation by grace through faith and the free exercise of human will. In fact, it appears that he sees the will to resist temptation as operative only for the person in whom the Holy Spirit is at work.

His exhortation does not stop with generalities. In Romans 6:13, he specifies, "Do not offer the parts of your body to sin, as instruments of wickedness, but rather offer yourselves to God, as those who have been brought from death to life; and offer the parts of your body to him as instruments of righteousness." The redeemed human will is anything but powerless. It can both say no to sinful temptation and say yes to the intent of God. With it, we can control even the individual parts of the body, some of which (like the tongue; James 3:3-12) are hard to tame. If the redeemed will is not in control, then sin is. And Paul ends this section with the combined affirmation and demand, "For sin shall not be your master, because you are not under law, but under grace" (Romans 6:14). We have come a long way from the opening question. Not only is it absurd to think about sinning so that grace may increase, but grace is precisely the reason that sin is not in charge of our lives.

This brings us to the next argument, which begins with the question, "Shall we sin because we are not under law but under grace?" (Romans 6:15). The former section would have prepared the reader to reject such a notion in general, but this form of the question permits Paul to deal with the false contrast between law and grace. Law and grace are not alternatives. It is not necessary to reject one in order to accept the other. The true alternatives in life are sin and obedience or sin and God. Verse 16 shows that slavery and freedom are also false alternatives. One cannot really choose freedom—only which master one is to serve. "Doing your own thing" is not freedom; it is slavery to sin. We should note the importance in this verse and the next of the term *obedience,* a term that we noticed in Romans 1:5 and that we'll see used again in chapters 15 and 16. For Paul, there is no such thing as passive Christianity. Either it is translated into active living or it is an illusion. A major characteristic of a servant is obedience to the master; so the Christians as servants are "slaves . . . to obedience, which leads to righteousness" (Romans 6:16).

In this verse (Romans 6:17), Paul breaks into a characteristic prayer of thanksgiving. (See Romans 7:25; 1 Corinthians 15:57; 2 Corinthians 2:14; 8:16; 9:15; 2 Timothy 1:3.) In this way, he makes it clear that he is not so much criticizing his Roman readers as laying out before them his understanding of the Christian message and life in such a way as to point up the similarities with their understanding. The change he is outlining here between the old life of sin and the new life in Christ is the very change they themselves had experienced. For that, both he and they are grateful to God. Furthermore, when he writes, "You wholeheartedly obeyed the form of teaching to which you were entrusted" (Romans 6:17), he uses the same verb he used in a negative sense in Romans 1:24, 26, and 28. Here, it is translated "entrusted"; in the earlier passage, it described people given over to sin. Here, Paul gives thanks that the Roman believers have given themselves over to the Christian teaching. The result is simply stated in verse 18, "You have been set free from sin and have become slaves to righteousness."

Paul opens verse 19 with a self-conscious statement about his use of language to help finite human beings to understand: "I put this in human terms because you are weak in your natural selves." This he follows with an exhortation for them as people who used to offer their bodies in "slavery to impurity and to ever-increasing wickedness," to offer them in "slavery to righteousness leading to holiness." He continues to use the slavery metaphor, since it allows him to use terms that would be especially vivid to readers in the first-century Roman empire, and especially in Rome, where a large segment of the population consisted of slaves. With this metaphor, then, Paul graphically describes the radical change that takes place when a person becomes a Christian. The change involves both status and responsibility. Even people who are not wholly divine, and thus have limitations, can show the change by putting themselves at the disposal of righteousness on the road to sanctification. This last term appears only here and in verse 22 in the epistle; yet Paul's emphasis on the results of justification and on the work of the Holy Spirit (especially in chapter 8) give the impression that holiness or sanctification plays an important role in his understanding of the Christian life. As will become even more apparent, his concept of sanctification is not one of perfectionism, but of the continuing work of new creation and preparation for perfection, which is carried on in the believer by the Holy Spirit. It is equally obvious that he sees the will of the believer as crucial to this process; otherwise he would hardly attach such a statement to an exhortation to action.

Romans 6:20-22 continues the structure of contrasts in the slavery metaphor. "When you were slaves to sin, you were free from the control of righteousness" (Romans 6:20). Once again, we see that the contrast is not between slavery and freedom, but between sin and righteousness, since slavery to one is freedom from the other.

At this point, Paul introduces the idea of benefit from the work done or from the relationship to the master. "What benefit did you reap at that time from the things you are now ashamed of?" he asks (Romans 6:21). He suggests that the only benefit was death. The contrast is then made with the Christian life: "But now that you have been set free from sin and have become slaves to God, the benefit you reap leads to holiness, and the result is eternal life" (Romans 6:22). Who wouldn't exchange shame and death for sanctification and eternal life? If the argument in verses 1-14, based on the reality of the Christian life, does not convince a person of the absurdity of mixing sinful acts with godly living, then surely this argument based on the results of the two contrasting life-styles should.

Romans 6:23 brings this part of the argument to a poetic conclusion by summarizing the logic and leaving the reader with a promise rooted in the Lord himself: "For the wages of sin is death, but the gift of God is eternal life in Christ Jesus our Lord." Even here, Paul cannot make a simple summary; he must show that the comparison itself is absurd. He does this by making the additional contrast of "wages" and "gift." With sin, the person gets what he or she deserves. With God, the person receives the gift of life, which is far beyond what anyone could earn or in any way deserve.

Once again, Paul indicates in this chapter the awesome reality and power of sin. He points out the close relationship (almost identification) of sin and death. He writes about both sin and death as playing the role of master to human beings who are their slaves. In fact, it seems that, as was true in chapter 5, he deals with sin/death as a personal reality working to counteract the creative righteousness of God by promoting disobedience, which leads to destruction.

Running through this otherwise pessimistic description of the human situation is the good news that sin/death is not necessarily in charge. In fact, the death and resurrection of Christ has crushed the power of sin and opened for humanity the option of righteousness and eternal life. We should be careful to consider this an option, since the will of the individual is a factor that removes it from the realm of certainty for every human being. The will works initially in the choice of faith—what Paul calls "the obedience of faith" (Romans 1:5; 16:26). This event, in which the power of God is unleashed in the life of the one who chooses to permit it, is identified by Paul in Romans 6:3, 4 as baptism.

In addition, even after baptism (which was the situation of the Roman readers), the will of the individual continues to be an important factor in the living of the gospel. Sin/death seems always to be ready to make another grand entrance into any life; so the Christian is to make those daily and detailed decisions about the parts of the body that will keep him or her in the service of God, doing acts of righteousness, which lead to eternal life. We have help in this matter of decision making, as we shall see in chapter 8; but we are responsible to make the decisions. Life is a gift of God, but we live with the necessity constantly to decide whether we are to follow God as our Master or to walk to our own destruction.

CHAPTER EIGHT

The Tension of the Christian Life

Romans 7:1-25

Romans 7 has been the focus of debate among students of Paul for centuries. It presents some especially troublesome questions about the apostle's understanding of the nature of humankind—his anthropology. One of the reasons the chapter has been problematic is the practice of scholars to treat it in isolation from the rest of the epistle, especially chapters 1, 2, and 5, which likewise treat anthropological issues. But chapter 7 is such a passionate description of the human situation that it must be studied carefully and fully if we are to grasp Paul's concept of humankind and the nature of the Christian life.

One other element in Paul's thinking that we shall be dealing with in this chapter is sin. This will not be surprising, since sin has been a major consideration in most of the chapters of Romans we have looked at up until now; but the personal way in which Paul handles the topic in this chapter makes it more than an issue—it makes it a personal problem. As we shall see, one of the main points of debate across the centuries has been whether or not Paul could have really been relating a personal experience here or whether he is using a vivid style for effect.

A major weakness of much writing and preaching on this chapter is, it seems to me, the practice of isolating it from chapter 8. The contrast between the two chapters is obvious to anybody who reads them; but this does not mean that they must be separated. On the contrary, in the light of the way Paul is using contrasts to make his point in Romans, we should hold the two chapters together so that the tension between them will lead us to the creative understanding Paul was trying to communicate.

In order to understand how this chapter fits into the argument of the epistle, we should review briefly the first six chapters. Paul's stated purpose in writing (Romans 1:8-15 and 2:16) is to introduce himself and his thinking to the Christians in Rome. Thus, we would expect to find a quite systematic treatment of the gospel. Romans 1:1-17 introduces the writer and his opening theme: the Christian gospel, in which a new righteousness of God is proclaimed. The need of humankind for this good news is dealt with in Romans 1:18—3:23, where he shows that all have sinned—pagan and Jew alike. Romans 3:24-26 states the heart of the gospel: the sacrificial death of Jesus, which in one stroke reveals the righteousness of God and redeems from the power of sin the person who receives this gift of righteousness by faith. Romans 3:27—4:25 shows the universality of this offer of redemption, since it is attainable not by law but by faith. Paul illustrates his point with the experience of Abraham. Romans 5:1-11 adds to the promise of justification and redemption the effects of salvation and reconciliation. Then, to point up the radical difference, he contrasts Adam and Christ in Romans 5:12-21, and, in so doing, deals with the entrance of sin into the world and its resultant death. Adam's sin permitted the entrance of sin as a power, but Christ's death broke the power of sin and resulted in life.

All of this outline of the gospel raises some questions, and Paul now deals with three of them, but in such a way as to answer the even more general question, "How does all this work in the individual life?" Chapter 6 answers the questions, "Shall we go on sinning so that grace may increase?" (verses 1-14) and, "Shall we sin because we are not under law but under grace?" (verses 15-23). While answering these questions directly, as we have seen, he proclaims that the power of sin and the law has been effectively broken by Christ, and that His victorious power is available to the one who in faith is baptized. This, he says, is the turning point from death to life, the entrance into the new reality that God has established through the death and resurrection of Christ.

Thus, Paul has already established that he and his readers are living in the new reality offered by God in Christ. We should expect now a description of his new life—how it affects our thinking and acting. The ethical passages of Romans 12—15 fit this expectation, as does his dealing with a new understanding of the place of Israel in chapters 9—11. Chapter 8 is definitely oriented to the present help and future promise of God's Holy Spirit in the life of the Christian. Chapter 7 confronts us with the big question. Does it break the progress of the letter and describe again the state of the person outside of Christ? Or can we understand it as sharing with chapters 8—15 the description of the new reality? I want to suggest that the latter is the better alternative. Let's see how Paul works out his reasoning.

The first six verses of the chapter offer an illustration of the principle that "the law has authority over a man only as long as he lives" (Romans 7:1). This is a theme that Paul mentioned in Romans 6:14, but had not really followed up on until now: that the grace of God frees the Christian not only from sin, but also from the law. Just as the Christian in baptism has died to sin, so the Christian has also died to the law, which, therefore, has no more jurisdiction over him or her.

To illustrate such a principle is bound to be difficult, since the death Paul speaks of is one the believer receives from Christ's death—the believer thus remaining actually alive. One can hardly imagine such a thing's happening in a human court of law, and therefore any human illustration is bound to be inadequate. So Paul contents himself with illustrating the more general principle, "Death effects a decisive change in respect of relationship to the law."[25]

Verse 4 makes it clear that Paul expects the illustration to do no more than that, although it does give him a connecting point for the further idea that this new freedom is an opportunity to give oneself to a new Master and bear fruit for Him. Therefore, the illustration is adequate if we do not make more demands than this upon it. The picture is simple: the married woman is bound by law to be faithful to her husband as long as he lives, but his death frees her from this law and permits her to marry another. Death, then, results in release, or freedom, from the law.

This brief illustration serves the same purpose in relation to the law as does the slavery illustration in Romans 6:15ff in relation to sin. It deals, then, with the same situation as does the latter half of chapter 6 and forms the transition to the discussion of the law in chapter 7. It is important for us to note at this point that this colorful transition indicates that what follows will not break the progress of the epistle, but should serve as another step forward.

---

[25]C. E. B. Cranfield, *A Critical and Exegetical Commentary on the Epistle to the Romans,* Volume 1 (Edinburgh: T. & T. Clark, 1975), p. 331.

As Paul applies his principle in verses 4-6, he restates what he has already written in Romans 6:5 about the Christian's connection with the death and resurrection of Jesus: "You also died to the law through the body of Christ, that you might belong to another, to him who was raised from the dead, in order that we might bear fruit to God" (Romans 7:4). This closing statement permits him to preach a little by reminding his audience of their responsibility to do more than just enjoy their most favored status with God. Romans 7:5 brings up the "sinful passions" with which he must deal in the rest of the chapter, but verse 6 sets the scene by reminding the reader that no matter how difficult life may seem, "we have been released" and we now "serve in the new way of the Spirit, and not in the old way of the written code."

Thus, we have in Romans 7:1-6 another example of Paul's ability to tie together themes treated in the last several chapters and to introduce themes to be dealt with later, while at the same time applying these ideas in the lives of his readers.

Verses 7-14a deal with the relationship of sin and law. From this point on to the end of the chapter, Paul's writing style is very personal. Up until now, he has used primarily the second and third persons and the first person plural; now he uses primarily the first person singular. This fact, coupled with the intensity of the content here, makes the identification of the person the most important and also the most difficult question in the interpretation of the chapter. The matter is further complicated by the abrupt change of tense from the past to the present at verse 14, and by the order of the two statements in verse 25. But trying not to anticipate those two factors, let us proceed in order through the passage.

Verse 7 picks up a question that could arise from the statements in Romans 5:20 ("The law was added so that the trespass might increase"), in Romans 6:14 ("For sin shall not be your master, because you are not under law"), and in the first six verses of this chapter. The question, "Is the law sin?" evokes the answer, "No, but...."

Paul develops the first half of his answer with a series of strong statements about the divine origin of the law. Since the law came from God (Romans 7:25), it cannot be identified with sin (Romans 7:7). It was intended to bring life (Romans 7:10). It shows the utter sinfulness of sin (Romans 7:13). It leads us to Christ. (See Galatians 3:19-25.) It is holy, righteous, and good (Romans

7:12, 16). And, perhaps for Paul's argument most important, it is spiritual (Romans 7:14).

The "but" half of his reply is more often recognized, since in both Romans and Galatians Paul is basically negative about the law. On the practical level, he points out that the law cannot accomplish justification because of the weakness of the flesh (Romans 3:20; 8:3). In fact, he points out, sin finds its foothold in the individual through the law (Romans 7:8). And furthermore, the law has been fulfilled, and thus its effectiveness for justification has been finished in Christ (Romans 10:4). But ineffectiveness alone cannot account for Paul's vehement rejection of the law here. He claims also that the law, in a personal sense, enslaves the individual (Galatians 4:3-9). This parallels what he says about sin in Romans 6. In fact, he insists that a return to the law is actually a return to idolatry (Galatians 4:1-10). To identify the keeping of the law with paganism must mean that Paul sees law as running counter to his gospel, since legalism tends to erect barriers between people that the gospel tries to break down.

It seems clear, then, that when Paul writes negatively about the law, he is referring to the observing of rules to earn status with God, a purpose and use of the law that was not intended by its giver. It is obvious to Paul as a believer in Christ that God did not intend His law as the final means of His self-revelation and His redemption. Therefore, the law itself is good, since it comes from God, but it becomes a problem for human beings when we try to claim more for it than God intended.

This sort of dialectic understanding of the law demands an explanation, and that is what Paul offers in Romans 7:7-11. Note that the commandment he chooses as an example is the one that relates to the inner person. Then he further generalizes it by leaving off the qualifying objects listed in Exodus 20:17 and Deuteronomy 5:21. In verse 8, Paul pictures sin as gaining a bridgehead or foothold through the law and producing all kinds of covetousness in him. It appears that sin is involved in a military-style operation against the person, and once the bridgehead has been established, the march from desire to sinful act and on to death is irreversible. The law, intended to defend against sin, becomes in this scenario at best a means of recognizing sin, while at the same time drawing attention to it. The law is not sin, but the individual is practically passive and defenseless in the face of the onslaught of sin.

As was pointed out earlier, Paul here begins to use primarily the first person singular. In the Greek language, it is hardly necessary to use a pronoun as the subject of a sentence, since the form of the verb indicates the person acting. But beginning in verse 9, Paul uses his first person singular pronoun (which in Greek is *ego)* repeatedly. It is used eight times in chapter 7 and not at all in chapter 8. The opening statement here is rather surprising: "Once I was alive apart from law" (Romans 7:9). This connection with life and death, along with several other less obvious themes, reminds the careful reader that Paul could hardly deal with the reality of sin apart from his understanding of Genesis 3. There also, we find the original life of purity and innocence, the giving of a commandment, the use of that command by the serpent to deceive the person, the desire, the act of disobedience, and death. Paul seems to have used the original fall into sin as a pattern for his and every other person's fall. (See also Romans 5:12). The point of Romans 7:9 is simply that before the commandment makes one conscious of sin and guilt, the individual lives an unencumbered existence. But once the reception of the law arouses one's responsibility with regard to sin, life is ruled by death.

Here it becomes clear that Paul is using the concepts of life and death in what we would call a spiritual sense. At the same time, we dare not separate this understanding of death from the physical reality. It appears in chapter 5 and also in Romans 6:23 that the result of sin is the ultimate loss of life, immediately in this spiritual sense, but in the end a total death. Paul does not deal here or elsewhere with the question of whether or not humankind was created immortal; he merely deals with the fact of death, experienced and expected by all, since all have sinned.

Romans 7:10 continues Paul's defense of the law with the confession that its intent was life but that, in his experience, it brought death. How? Verse 11 makes sin the culprit—the subject of the verse. He repeats here his military idiom from verse 8: sin, having established a bridgehead by the commandment, "deceived me, and through the commandment put me to death." The word here translated "deceived" is the same word that appears in the Greek translation (the Septuagint) of Genesis 3:13. Here, it is sin instead of the serpent that deceives and kills. Thus, Paul can maintain in verse 12 that "the law is holy, and the commandment is holy, righteous and good," since sin was in the world before the law. (See Romans 5:13.) Verse 13 in chapter 7 goes on to explain that the purpose of this process of death is to allow sin to be recognized as utterly sinful.

We see, then, midway through the chapter, several elements of Paul's understanding of humankind—at least as they apply to the individual without or before Christ:

1. Before the recognition of sin, which the law brings, one is alive.

2. One's acceptance of the law as command to be obeyed permits sin—the powerful enemy—to gain a foothold.

3. Sin, once it enters the life of a person, is such a powerful influence in the flesh that one can say, "I died" (Romans 7:10), or that we were "in the flesh," so that the passions of sin were so in control that we produced fruit only to death.

4. Once the force of sin moves into the human's life, the individual is powerless against it and unable to accomplish anything good.

Verse 14 begins a passionate description of the experience of the power of sin in the life of the individual. Paul begins with another statement in support of the law, but one that foreshadows an emphasis to be expanded in chapter 8 and stands in contrast to the ego statements to follow: "the law is spiritual." But the next statement has elicited an ongoing debate among interpreters: "But I am unspiritual, sold as a slave to sin." The word translated "unspiritual" in this version really means "fleshly." The tense is present now. The ego is in a place of emphasis in the sentence, as is the verb *am*. The normal understanding would be that Paul is describing his present situation.

But the strongly negative language he uses in the description that follows raises doubts in the minds of many people that he could have been that pessimistic about the Christian experience. The fact that the passage contains no mention of Christ or the Holy Spirit until verse 25 and that it follows without transition the preceding verses, which clearly deal with the human experience without Christ, raises serious questions.

What we have here is either a description of a person without Christ, using the first person singular pronoun and the present tense as rhetorical devices, or a description of a real struggle within the Christian, or else some compromise between the two, if that is possible. We should probably admit from the outset that no position will solve all the difficulties.

Let's take seriously the natural meaning of the sentences and see whether it is understandable as a description of at least a continuing possibility for the Christian. Could Paul as a Christian say, "I am unspiritual"? Chapter 8, which is usually used as an argument against this possibility, gives us the key by putting the whole Christian life—indeed the whole of creation—in the framework of the ultimate end and judgment of the world. Paul indicates there that the whole creation is groaning until the end. He proclaims that there is no condemnation for the Christian, but he never claims any lack of tension. He says we are free of the dominion of sin, that we are no longer living in the flesh (Romans 8:9); but at the same time, he warns his readers against the possibility (verses 12, 13) of living according to the flesh. He explicitly admits (Romans 8:18) that the Christian suffers, and then compares that suffering with labor pains—internal suffering. The whole picture, as realistic as one can draw it, points to the time when this new reality in Christ will be fulfilled; but not yet.

Now let's return to Romans 7:14-20. Paul says he is fleshly and then adds "sold as a slave to sin" (Romans 7:14). This takes up again the theme of the complete dominance of sin. But Paul has already described the state of the Christian as "set free from sin and . . . slaves to God" (Romans 6:22). How could he now say that a Christian is sold as a slave to sin? This cannot describe a Christian in a healthy fellowship with God. And as Philippians 3:6 shows, neither can it be an objective description of Paul's experience of the law as a Jew, since he saw himself then as "faultless." The closest parallel appears to be Galatians 4:3, where Paul (from the standpoint of his Christian experience) describes the experience that he and the Galatians had formerly shared under the law as that of children "in slavery under the basic principles of the world." The difference is, of course, that the Galatians statement is clearly in the past tense, while Romans 7:14ff is present. If the tense is insignificant here, then Paul could be speaking about his former experience as a Jew. We should, however, bear in mind that his purpose in Galatians was to give a very explicit warning for the Christians not to return to this bondage to the law, and he contrasts that possibility with their experience of the Holy Spirit. Is this not precisely the contrast he makes in Romans 7 and 8? As we shall see, there are additional similarities between the two passages.

No interpretation of the first person singular and present tense in our passage is without difficulties. But it seems to me that the most likely possibility is that Paul is using himself as a representative of the believing individual who is trying to win God's favor by achieving righteousness for himself. Paul characteristically warned Christians against this sort of fall from grace into works righteousness. In 1 Corinthians 1:18—2:16, he defined grace over against wisdom—intellectual elitism. In 2 Corinthians, he seemed to be battling Judaizers again. A similar struggle is visible in Philippians 3:2—4:1. Several of these concerns of Paul come together later in Colossians 2:6-23, where human attainments and regulations of both Judaism and paganism are rejected as valid criteria for a relationship with God. Romans 7 seems to be the most intense of these statements, but it is certainly not isolated from the rest of Paul's concerns. Thus, Paul's statement in Romans 7:14 is a strongly rhetorical description of a situation in which individuals cannot help themselves.

This helplessness deepens in Romans 7:15 as Paul states that he does not know what he is doing. He offers one small consolation in verse 16: at least the desire to do good indicates his agreement that the law is good. In verse 17, Paul returns to the conclusion that the very personal and powerful reality of sin has taken over and overrules him.

Verses 18-20 repeat most of this, emphasizing again the total slavery of the actions to sin. He qualifies this, however, in verse 18, where he says, "Nothing good lives in me, that is, in my sinful nature." He wants to insist that his intentions are good. Thus, there is some division of the person here. The will is not in control, but it wants the good. The flesh (sinful nature), on the other hand, has become the place where sin is at home and displaying its power.

Since a major part of the argument in the crucial chapter 8 hinges on the contrast between flesh and spirit, it is important here to look at Paul's use of the term *flesh*. The New International Version translates the Greek word *sarx* in most instances as "sinful nature." It appears twenty-six times in Romans, thirteen times in chapter 8 alone. In most cases where this Greek word is used in the Greek translation of the Old Testament (the Septuagint), it translates a word that refers to the physical makeup of a human being or animal. A few times, it refers to a blood relationship. Both uses are basically neutral. It was the Greek philosophers who gave flesh a negative connotation, when they contrasted it with the soul or the mind, insisting that the soul was the good part of a person or that the life of the mind was the highest good. But the Bible generally, while taking the reality of evil very seriously, does not characterize the physical aspect of humankind as naturally sinful. To do so would raise questions about God's wisdom and authority in creation.

In harmony with this prevailing view found in the Bible, Paul remains neutral in his use of the term *flesh*. We find him using it in a negative sense at times, but making it clear through his grammar or modifiers that he did not consider flesh evil in itself. W. D. Davies explains, "The term *sarx* denoted for Paul the material element in man which is morally indifferent; it has, however, become the basis from which sin attacks man; has, in short, passed under the dominion of sin. . . ."[26] This position agrees basically with the attitude displayed in most of the Jewish rabbinical comments, as well as in the documents called the Dead Sea Scrolls.

We should also bear in mind that Paul's use of *flesh* in Romans is more negative than in the Pauline literature at large. He has apparently decided to use this term in contrast to *spirit* as his argument develops. But we shall see that he tempers this negative connotation time and time again—even in chapter 8.

Up to chapter 8, we find the word used in five different senses: to denote a racial relationship (Romans 1:3; 4:1), as the physical body (Romans 2:28), as humankind in general (Romans 3:20), as a designation of weakness (Romans 6:19), and as the stage of sin (Romans 7:5, 18, 25). Chapter 8 does not go beyond this range of understanding, but rather accepts it and discusses its ramifications. It is clear that human life is more than flesh, so that those who live according to the flesh (Romans 8:4, 5, 12, 13) or in the flesh (Romans 8:8, 9) or with their minds set on the flesh (Romans 8:5, 6, 7) cannot please God (Romans 8:8), concentrating thus on the, at best, powerless part of human existence.

Of the remaining five appearances of the word in this letter, four (Romans 9:3, 5, 8; 11:14) designate the Jewish race, and the remaining one (Romans 13:14), the flesh as the seat of the lusts, to

---

[26]W. D. Davies, *Paul and Rabbinic Judaism* (Philadelphia: Fortress Press, 1980), p. 19.

which we should not surrender. Thus, Paul views the flesh as vulnerable to temptation and certainly to be subjected to the spirit; but he displays little of the judgmental dualism of the Greek philosophers whose doctrines were believed by so many of his day. *Flesh* is Paul's way of expressing the responsibility of the individual for his or her sins without completely identifying the ego and sin.

Paul's use of the term *flesh* thus sets the stage for his picture of tension in the individual. This is portrayed most graphically in the last five verses of the chapter. In verse 21, he claims that his experience is that, as a general rule, "when I want to do good, evil is right there with me." This statement recapitulates in personal terms what he has been saying throughout the chapter.

Verse 22 introduces another term, *inner being,* which describes an aspect of human experience. Paul delights in God's law in his inner being—or, as it is sometimes translated, "inner man." The term appears in only two other texts of Paul: 2 Corinthians 4:16 and Ephesians 3:16, and in both cases it refers to that part of the person that is continually being renewed and strengthened by the Holy Spirit. In this passage, it could refer back to his use of *conscience* in Romans 2:14, 15 and thus mean the moral person. But it seems to me that it is more closely related here to the mind, which, according to Romans 1:28, was corrupted by sin, but which here (in verses 23 and 25) struggles against sin and serves God's law, and in Romans 12:2 should be continually renewed to effect the transformation of the dedicated Christian.

This connection is emphasized by verse 23, where he describes "another law at work in the members of my body, waging war against the law of my mind and making me a prisoner of the law of sin at work within my members." It seems clear that the other law in his members is the law (principle or power) of sin and that *members* here is equivalent to the *flesh*—the area where sin is at home in us. The positive side of the statement is the will to do good, the delight in God's law (see Psalm 119) in the inner being and here in the mind. We should note that what Paul is describing here is not some abstract concept of dualism, where the flesh and the spirit are constantly at war in every human being, but rather a united person (ego) who has become a battleground for the cosmic struggle between the powers of good and evil. The antagonists here are not parts of the person, but God and sin. The field of battle is the ego; the opposing camps are the flesh and the mind. The prize is the human being—you and I. We note also that the whole description is in the present tense, which (it seems to me) is more than a matter of writing style.

As we look once again at this chapter alongside chapters 1 and 2, we see that Paul assumed that human beings are created with a will to do good. But according to Romans 1:20 and 28, this good will is buried by sin and made inoperative. The mind thus becomes depraved. But in Romans 7:23, the mind is once again aligned with God. Sin has been pushed into the flesh. This sets the stage for the cry for help (not despair or hopelessness) in verse 24 and the cry of victorious thanks in 25. The three Greek words that are translated by the first sentence of verse 24, "What a wretched man I am," are hard to make sense of, since none of them is a verb. They do not form a neat sentence; but they do express a passionate cry: "Miserable I man!" The picture of the internal struggle of this ego that we have seen makes it easy to understand that he is miserable and looking for deliverance from his condition, which can best be described as death. The "I man" is in trouble, but the answering cry is, "Thanks be to God—through Jesus Christ our Lord!" The Deliverer has come, and He will ultimately deliver.

For those who insist that Paul could not be referring here to the experience of a Christian, the last part of verse 25 presents a problem. The first half is seen as the proclamation of delivery. Why, then, should Paul return to a description of the tension? But the verse can be accepted as a very honest statement of the tension in the life of the person who tries to do the will of God by his or her own power. It thus becomes a bridge to chapter 8, with the summary, "I myself in my mind am a slave to God's law, but in the sinful nature a slave to the law of sin." Chapter 8, as we shall see, presents a completely different picture; it is a proclamation of victory. The big difference, however, is not in reference to human nature, but in reference to the Holy Spirit and the coming judgment. Whereas in chapter 7, the struggle takes place between the flesh and the mind; in chapter 8, it is between the flesh and the Holy Spirit. The Spirit of God is the One who makes victory possible. Chapter 7 shows the believer wanting and trying to do good, but failing because this ego cannot do it alone. Chapter 8 shows the result of the presence of the Holy Spirit.

I once heard of a very wise preacher whose first advice to a young woman whom he had just baptized was, "Now go home and read Romans 7." That is exactly what Paul had in mind. Every Christian needs to be constantly reminded of the ever-present danger of temptation. Sin is most potent in the life of the believer who forgets that he or she is always and totally dependent on the power of God to win the battle. We would be wise never to read Romans 8 without Romans 7—or the other way around.

CHAPTER NINE

The Victory of the Christian Life

Romans 8:1-39

Whole books have been published on this one chapter, and it is certainly tempting to a preacher or teacher to wax eloquent at this point, since there is so much here that is both profound and poetic. Yet, as has already been noted, there is a danger in treating chapter 8 apart from chapter 7. One of the grand attractions of chapter 8 is its positive note—its undying optimism. But our careful analysis of chapter 7 should keep us aware that Paul was looking with his eyes wide open to the total reality of life as we know it. For most of us, chapter 7 is more descriptive of present experience than chapter 8, but the latter presents a vision that nourishes our hope for this life and the life to come.

Romans 8:1-17 picks up a number of threads of Paul's gospel from former chapters and weaves them into a background for the strong statements in verses 19-22. Following this, verses 26-39 use graphic terminology to summarize and apply the chapter's main line of thought.

And what is this main topic? Because of the twenty-two appearances of the term *spirit,* as compared with only five previous appearances in the epistle, many conclude that the topic here is the Spirit or life in the Spirit. But a closer reading shows that the reality of, and life in, the Spirit, along with a number of other thoughts, are used by Paul to undergird his main point. Chapter 7 has described vividly the tension in which the Christian lives—a tension partly caused by, and totally illuminated by, the entrance through baptism into the life in Christ, which he has described in chapter 6. The question remains: why has God condemned us to this life of tension? Chapter 8 is Paul's attempt to support his reply: "Therefore, there is now no condemnation for those who are in Christ Jesus" (Romans 8:1). His major concern is, then, the assurance of salvation in light of the difficulties of the Christian life. His aim seems to be to develop in his readers confidence in the ultimate victory of the Christ in whom they live.

The natural outline of the chapter is as follows:

1. The Life in the Spirit, verses 1-11
2. The Life of God's Children, verses 12-17
3. The Glory That Will Be, verses 18-30
4. The Confidence in Christ, verses 31-39.

The Life in the Spirit (8:1-11)

Romans 8:1 states the theme of the chapter (the security of salvation) negatively, and then the next ten verses proceed to contrast the life in the Spirit with the life oriented to the flesh. In the original Greek, Paul makes the connections within these verses clear by beginning his statements in verses 2, 3, 5, and 6 with the same conjunction (translated into English with either "for" or "because"). This clear series of arguments gives believers places where they can get a firm grip on their salvation.

The first of these is in the theme statement itself, where Paul reminds his readers that the reality of the situation for Christians is that they are "in Christ Jesus." This is Paul's characteristic way of referring to what it means to be a Christian. He normally uses either the preposition *in* or some compound word that indicates a close relationship (*fellow-workers,* for instance) and in this way reminds followers of Christ that the Lord is in the struggle with them. The relationship between the disciple and the Lord is so close that language can only describe it approximately. Furthermore, Paul usually just states the case; it is a reality in spite of the fact that the individual very often does not "feel" that way at all. Being a Christian is not dependent on feeling like a Christian, since one becomes a Christian by the Lord's initiative and one remains a Christian by that same power and authority. According to Paul's writings, the reality of the presence of the Lord is not dependent on the believer's feelings at the moment. Christians are "in Christ" or "with Christ" according to His promise and initiative; the believers' choice, then, is what to do about it or how to display this reality in their lives.

The second grip Paul offers is the Spirit. As we noted above, he has used this term twenty-two times in this chapter. It appears only thirty-five times in the whole epistle. So there is no escaping an attempt to understand the Spirit if we are to understand Romans, and especially chapter 8. The word can mean wind or breath in addition to spirit in both Greek and Hebrew; so Paul is using a term that works the same in both of his main languages. The overriding characteristic of *spirit* in the Old Testament is power—the power of creation (Genesis 1:2), the power of prophecy (Isaiah 61:1), and special powers given at certain times for leadership or aid of one sort or another (Judges 3:10). This use of the word appears alongside its use as a term to denote the inner person. So Paul could speak of both the spirit of an individual and the Spirit of God. There are times even in this chapter where it is difficult to decide which point of reference he has in mind, but in most instances, he is clearly referring to the Holy Spirit.

It is interesting to note the changing way Paul uses the term *spirit* in chapter 8. In verse 2, he makes his connection with chapter 7 when he claims that "the law of the Spirit of life set me free from the law of sin and death." In verse 4, he draws on his usage in chapter 7 of *flesh* as the stage of sin and draws a sharp contrast between living "according to the sinful nature" (flesh) and living "according to the Spirit." Verse 3 has identified the flesh as weak but also as the nature in which God's Son came to overcome sin, thus condemning sin in the flesh. This makes it possible for the believer to break the old pattern and walk according to (or in the sphere of) the Spirit. Verse 5 further defines this life-style as a mind-set, and verse 6 completes the contrast with the claim that the mind-set of the flesh is death, but the mind-set of the Spirit is life and peace. The negative side of this claim is further explained in verses 7 and 8. Then verse 9 introduces the phrase *in the Spirit* in contrast with *in the flesh,* a construction that is hidden by the NIV translation: "You, however, are controlled not by the sinful nature but by the Spirit, if the Spirit of God lives in you." Certainly being "in the Spirit" implies control, but there must be more to it than that. Verses 10 and 11 are made up of a series of statements in which no attempt is made to be systematic or even consistent. Being in the spirit means that "the Spirit of God lives in you," that "the Spirit of him who raised Jesus Christ is living in you," and that "he who raised Christ from the dead will also give life to your mortal bodies through his Spirit, who lives in you." And in the middle of these statements stands one more usage of *spirit* (verse 10), "But if Christ is in you, your body is dead because of sin, yet your spirit is alive because of righteousness." Thus, this complex statement becomes a proclamation of hope for

the total human—both body and spirit—a hope made possible by
the fact of the believer's living in the sphere of the Spirit by means
of God's gracious act of justification.

(3) A third handle Paul offers the Christian here is his contrast
between the Spirit and the flesh. The problem so vividly described
in chapter 7 is the weakness of the flesh, or our vulnerability to
sin in the flesh. Here in chapter 8, Paul shows clearly that the
weakness of the flesh is hardly worth comparing with the power
of God's Spirit. Even the number of times Paul uses the word
spirit impresses the reader with the extreme contrast. The end
of the matter is pronounced by God's clear statement in the
resurrection. Since God has done that, we can trust Him to
take care of the problem of our human flesh, also—especially
in the light of the fact that He chose human flesh as the means
by which to gain the victory (Romans 8:3). In all of this,
Paul is careful never to indicate that human flesh is bad in
itself. It is part of God's creation. It has become the stage of sin,
but God has made it also the stage of redemption from sin. In
the act of redemption—the crucifixion and resurrection of
Christ—God has established once and for all that life is more
powerful than death. Even though we Christians continue to live
surrounded by death, we have the experience of life and the assurance of life everlasting.

The Life of God's Children (8:12-17)

In this paragraph, Paul gives us a strong exhortation to live in a
way appropriate to the reality of redemption. It is parallel to the
statement in Galatians 5:16-27, another contrast between life according to the flesh and life empowered by the Spirit. Again we
see (Romans 8:12) that Paul recognizes the tension within the
believer between the competing obligations of the flesh and the
Spirit. It is important that we Christians remember that, even
living in the Spirit, not everything that seems natural is right.
Even though the Christian has died to sin, the possibility of its
practice—indeed the strong temptation—is still very real and must
continually be "put to death" (Romans 8:13). The new creation
does not destroy the fallen creation, but rather restores the relationship with the Creator in which we can share the power necessary to destroy the works of sin. The Spirit gives the Christian the
power to say no to the sinful practices of the body when he or she
is tempted to do them.

This restored relationship Paul describes as "sonship" (Romans 8:15). This is the same intimate relationship to which Jesus testified in His prayers by His use of the familiar form of address, "*Abba,* Father." One of the most striking contrasts in the whole epistle is the one between being "sold as a slave to sin" (Romans 7:14) and the fact that "we are God's children" (Romans 8:16). The implications of this adoption are staggering: we are "heirs of God and coheirs with Christ," which implies also a "[sharing] in his sufferings in order that we may also share in his glory" (Romans 8:17).

Here is the climax of the paragraph, with the term *glory* once again pulling the strands together into a whole. *Glory* refers to the image of God in which Adam was created, the glory Adam lost as a result of the fall, the glory of God, which each sinner lacks (Romans 3:23), the glory of the life that Jesus led, and the glory for which we may hope (Romans 5:2). Thus Paul, with this promise of glorification, reaches back to original creation, deals with the reality of new creation, and looks forward to the restoration of God's purpose in creation—a restoration that awaits the final judgment.

The Glory That Will Be (8:18-30)

If Paul is to speak about glorification, he must somehow defend his hope against the reality of present sufferings. This seeming contradiction must have been a constant challenge to the early church. First Peter 4:12—5:1, 10 deals with the same question in reference to glory. Just how does Paul deal with it? This passage is usually broken after verse 27; but it seems to me that verses 18-30 form a well-organized and tightly-reasoned unit. Verse 18 states the proposition, "I consider that our present sufferings are not worth comparing with the glory that will be revealed in us." This is followed by three statements that offer warrants or evidence for the proposition (verses 19-22, 23-25, and 26, 27) and a conclusion (29, 30). Each of the warrant statements is accompanied by a supporting statement and an implication. So this section is a very neatly-constructed piece of reasoning that makes a very important point.

The Evidence of Creation (19-22)

The first warrant offers the whole creation as a witness for Paul's contention. Verses 19-22 describe vividly the unity of humanity and the rest of creation. He makes clear here that sin has had an impact not only on human beings but also on the whole of the created universe. Not only is there lack of present fulfillment and longing for some future redemption in the human experience, but this same description fits the rest of creation also. "The creation waits in eager expectation for the sons of God to be revealed" (Romans 8:19). Paul's poetic mode of expression here highlights the intensity he sees in the present status of creation. It is waiting with muscles straining to catch a glimpse of what is coming and to lean toward it. The apostle has shown in chapter 1 that the basic sin involves the worship of the creation instead of the Creator; so he has already shown an intimate relationship between human sin and the physical universe. Now it becomes clear that, as a result of sin, the universe has been afflicted and so needs and anticipates the final end of sin. In other words, the fall of humanity from God's intent for the race has kept the rest of creation from its intended purpose, and the restoration of humanity to the status of children of God will be redemptive also for the rest of creation.

Verse 20 focuses on one aspect of the result of sin on the creation: "For the creation was subjected to frustration, not by its own choice, but by the will of the one who subjected it, in hope." The word translated "frustration" is characteristically used in a negative way by Paul. His point of reference for his usage here is most likely Ecclesiastes 1:2, "'Meaningless! Meaningless!' says the Teacher. 'Utterly meaningless! Everything is meaningless.'" The Greek word translated "frustration" in our Romans passage is the very word used by the Greek translators of the Ecclesiastes passage to render what is in the NIV translated "meaningless." Other words suggested as good equivalents are *vanity, emptiness,* and *purposelessness.* Whatever the best word is, it is clear that Paul sees the whole of creation out of order as a result of the sin of humanity.

Commentators argue over what he means by "the one who subjected it." The immediate cause of the frustration of creation was the sin of Adam; so in a formal way, Adam subjected it. But the real agent must have been God. Surely this is the sense of Genesis 3:17-19, where God curses the ground because of Adam. Furthermore, only God could subject it "in hope," which is Paul's main contention here. There is no hint that the Creator has lost control of His creation. Just the opposite is spelled out here and in verse 28, both of which should be compared with Colossians 1:17.

It is regrettable that *in hope* was not counted as the beginning of verse 21 when the Bible was divided into verses (centuries after the writing of the epistle). These two words act as a transition between the past and the future of creation. The affirmation reaches back to the eager expectation of verse 19 and pulls us into the substance of the future in verse 21. For Paul, hope signifies and unites many of the basic beliefs of his Jewish and Christian traditions. But hope is not wishful thinking; it has a specific object (here, the liberation of creation) and a firm foundation in the person of the Creator. As a result of our sin, God subjected the otherwise innocent creation to frustration on the basis of the hope (expectation) that humankind's redemption would result in creation's liberation.

Paul's goal in verse 21 is to contrast the present state of the creation (bondage to decay) with the glory of the future. The negative assessment of the creation at present is essentially a restatement of the frustration description in verse 20. The positive side of the sentence is an interesting series of nouns in the original, which sounds awkward when translated literally into English: "Into the freedom of the glory of the children of God." The problem with most English translations is that they transform *glory* into an adjective, when in the original it is the main noun. (The New International Version, for example, translates it, "Into the glorious freedom of the children of God.") Since we have already surveyed the use of *glory* in chapters 1, 3, and 5, we can now see the end of Paul's argument. The glory with which humanity was endowed in original creation, which was lost as a result of sin, and which we may hope for in Christ, is that state (akin to original creation) for which the creation longs, since it means freedom from the frustration in which every creature exists because of sin. Finally, since the sin of the human race caused the problem in the first place, it will be the redemption of the human race (now designated as "the children of God") that will make possible the freedom of the whole creation.

C. E. B. Cranfield seems to capture Paul's thought here when he writes, "the liberty proper to the creation is indeed the possession of its own proper glory—that is, of the freedom fully and perfectly to fulfill its Creator's purpose for it, that freedom which it does not have, so long as man, its lord, is in disgrace."[27] The final glory will be revealed in us (Romans 8:18), our revelation as children of God is what the creation awaits (Romans 8:19), and the creation will be freed precisely into that glory (Romans 8:21). No wonder then, that the whole creation groans and travails! Verse 22 brings this assertion of the witness of creation to a conclusion. Environmental pain, which was seen by many in Paul's tradition as a symbol of the coming of the glorious future or of some fearful happening (Isaiah 26:17; 66:7ff; Jeremiah 22:23; Hosea 13:13f; Mark 13:8), is used here to emphasize hope, which is made clear by the words "up to the present time" and the statement's close relationship with verse 18, which reminds us that "our present sufferings are not worth comparing with the glory that will be revealed in us."

The Evidence of Christian Experience (23-25)

The second warrant Paul offers for his affirmation in verse 18 is the voice of the experience of the Christian life. In verses 23-25, Paul points out that we share the longing of the creation. The Spirit is depicted here as being given as a sort of down payment in a business transaction, which indicates that there is much more to come. What we await is the fulness of the relationship with God and the freedom from sin. It is worth noting here that for Paul, freedom from sin and complete access to God does not mean what we usually hear described as a "spiritual existence." It is "our bodies" that are redeemed and not our souls from our bodies. Once again, we see that the Biblical hope is the resurrection of the human body, not some sort of disembodied existence of the soul. As in verse 11, we are reminded again that the resurrection of Jesus means the eternal life of identifiable individuals. In fact, as 1 Corinthians 15:44 shows, bodylessness is for Paul nonsense even in the resurrection.[28] We shall be delivered from fleshliness—from the power of sin, which has used our flesh for evil purposes—and that will mean the redemption of our bodies, that is, our total selves.

---

[27]Cranfield, Vol. 1, p. 331.

[28]W. D. Davies, *Paul and Rabbinic Judaism* (London: SPCK, 1958), p. 19.

Verses 24 and 25 affirm that hope is in the condition in which the Christian (along with the rest of creation—see verses 21 and 22) lives. This does not make the experience of suffering unreal or meaningless; it merely points us to something infinitely more glorious and important. It gives meaning to suffering by showing that suffering points to something else. It should be obvious to every Christian that all tears are not yet wiped away, that physical and mental pain are still very much part of our existence, and that the consummation of our salvation has not yet arrived. We live in the time of "not yet." For most people on our planet, this status quo leads either to extreme selfishness or to despair. For those who believe in the resurrected Christ, however, it leads us to confess, "In this hope we were saved. But hope that is seen is no hope at all. Who hopes for what he already has? But if we hope for what we do not yet have, we wait for it patiently" (Romans 8:24, 25). Such a testimony is not easy, since the pain experienced in a universe out of order is real for everybody in that universe. But our faith in the resurrected Lord gives us hope for the resurrection, which Paul has described in verse 21 as "the freedom of the glory of the children of God." So that faith and hope give meaning even to the experiences of life that are twisted by the power of sin in this fallen universe, since they remind us of "the glory that will be revealed in us" (Romans 8:18).

The Evidence of the Holy Spirit (26, 27)

Paul's third warrant for his proposition is the work of the Holy Spirit in the life of the Christian, as he describes it in verses 26 and 27: "In the same way, the Spirit helps us in our weakness." The Christian is pictured here as a part of fallen creation. It is, of course, no revelation to us that we have weaknesses, especially weaknesses in our prayer lives. All too often, "we do not know what [or how] we ought to pray." At that point, Paul proclaims, we can be assured that the Holy Spirit steps in. It is hardly necessary to speculate that Paul has in mind here the praying in tongues that he discusses elsewhere (see 1 Corinthians 14). He is merely assuring the Christian who is discouraged with the quality of his or her prayers that God's own Spirit is involved in the process of praying and God understands better than we what we want to ask, "because the Spirit intercedes for the saints in accordance with God's will." Whatever translation is necessary to make our prayers effective, we can rest assured that the translator, the Holy

Spirit, is able to state them even better than we could. This does not lessen the importance of prayer; it merely indicates that the effect of prayer does not rest entirely on our ability to state things well. Thank God for that!

Conclusion (28-30)

Verses 28-30 form a conclusion for the argument that began in verse 18. The three warrants have been presented, and now Paul can affirm on behalf of all believers, "We know that in all things God works for the good of those who love him, who have been called according to his purpose" (Romans 8:28). Since Paul's thought has covered such a vast expanse in this chapter, it is clear that his claim about "all things" here must encompass that same vastness. This is not just a literary devise; he is referring to the whole of creation, and also to the personalities and life experiences we all encounter along the way. Because of God's greatness, all things work together for good. This good is part of that glory that God has in store for those who love Him. Note that it is not those whom God loves who are the beneficiaries of this good. God loves all His creatures. But those who do not return His love are not in a position to accept His goodness.

Paul goes on to describe those who love God as those "who have been called according to his purpose." The Old Testament concept of the chosen people was always connected to a universal purpose (Genesis 12:2, 3) and such a calling was seen as so powerful that the God who calls is seen as the Creator of the people (Isaiah 43:1). The Christian should keep in mind that the God who redeems us in Christ Jesus is the Lord of the universe, who truly has "the whole world in His hands."

Verses 29 and 30 present the concepts of foreknowledge, predestination, call, justification, and glorification. These terms have puzzled readers and challenged theologians through the centuries. Too often, we fall into the trap of defining one without the other and then later trying to put them back together again. When we get to chapter 9, we shall take more time to deal with the issue of predestination, but for now it must suffice us to note that each of these terms can be shown to be connected in Jewish thinking with the act or power of creation, a connection that is clearly continued and developed in Christian thinking. What makes this connection possible for both Jew and Christian is the concept of God that underlies this and similar statements. God is here the

Creator-Lord of the universe, whose knowledge, power, and will control the flow of history to work out His purpose. That purpose had determined the character of creation, which has been thwarted by sin, and that purpose will restore that intended character to creation as sinners are "conformed to the likeness of his Son" (Romans 8:29). This restoration begins in the present, but will be fulfilled only in the final consummation. However He does it, God is in charge and will remain in charge of all of His creation.

The Confidence in Christ (8:31-39)

Here we come to one of the most stirring passages of the whole Bible. It accomplishes Paul's purpose of encouragement in a way that has made it a reference for Christians in times of difficulty throughout the history of the church. We have all discovered to some extent the truth of the description in chapter 7 of the inner turmoil that, at times, seems to be the overwhelming experience of life for the believer. We have also tasted the tension with the whole universe caused by the power of sin in the world. We all need to be convinced repeatedly, therefore, that "there is now no condemnation for those who are in Christ Jesus" (Romans 8:1) and that "our present sufferings are not worth comparing with the glory that will be revealed in us" (Romans 8:18). Paul has presented his arguments for these claims; now he calls the full orchestra of his rhetoric to join in a grand finale as he indicates with the opening question, "What, then, shall we say in response to this?"

This opening question suggests that what follows is a summary of what went before. In fact, it is sometimes argued that this passage is a conclusion to the whole context that begins with Romans 5:1. But it is obviously more than just a logical conclusion; it is a proclamation designed to arouse the determination of believers to remain faithful in spite of everything. Paul builds his case for confidence in a characteristic question-and-answer style. At first, he concentrates on rhetorical questions (Romans 8:31-33). These questions are asked in an important order. First, he draws our attention to the power and majesty of God—the Creator, who, as Paul has already established, is on our side. To live a victorious life, one hardly needs more than to know that God is for us. But there is more: God has done something that not only shows us that He is for us, but also accomplished what we needed to have done for us. He has redeemed us from sin through the gift of His Son, Jesus Christ. If He has gone that far, it is hardly sensible to think that he would then ignore us. So both the person of God and the salvation of God are offered to encourage us in what would otherwise be an impossibly hard life.

But the third question, a rhetorical question that reminds us of the absurdity of fear and discouragement, introduces a second series of statements, as well as one more question. This series, if we will allow ourselves to be carried along with it, can offer a profound insight and appreciation for what we have in Christ. Notice the order: "It is God who justifies." Paul has already identified God as the one "who justifies the wicked" (Romans 4:5). Since our salvation depends on Him and Him alone, nobody else has the right to bring any charge against us—not even we ourselves. But the next question persists, "Who is he that condemns?" The only possible answer is God himself or His Son; and that is precisely what Paul seems to say next, "Christ Jesus." If the sentence ended there, it would make perfect sense. He and He alone has the right to condemn sinful human beings, since, although not guilty of sin, He is the one who died for us. He has shown that it is possible to do the will of God perfectly while experiencing human life completely. Furthermore, He allowed himself to be killed in our place. Who has a better right to condemn? But there is more: He "was raised to life." Obviously, He could not really condemn anybody if He were not alive, but that is a minor consideration. What if I had been God and watched my Son die on that cross? What if I had watched the cruelty and then watched as they laid His body in a borrowed tomb? What if I had brought Him back to life? We can best understand what grace is when we realize that God could (and had every right to) have destroyed the human race on that first resurrection day, but instead, He used the power that overcame death for Jesus to make it possible for us to overcome death. Christ today "is at the right hand of God" (Romans 8:34). Notice that up until now, all of these statements about Jesus could be positive answers to the question, "Who is he that condemns?" Christ has the right; he has the power; he has the position to condemn. But what is he doing? He "is also interceding for us." The only one who is in a position to be the prosecuting attorney in our case has chosen to act as our defense attorney. Instead of condemning us, He is pleading for our salvation, not on the basis of any goodness of our own, but on the basis of His own righteous death and resurrection.

The rest of the chapter, then, is just one illustration after another of what the Christian need not fear. "Who shall separate us from the love of Christ?" (Romans 8:35). The kind of love that drove the Son of God to die and live for those responsible for His death is not going to let anybody or anything come between the lover and the beloved. Not even "trouble or hardship or persecution or famine or nakedness or danger or sword" can separate us from that love. It should be obvious that we can choose to live a life contrary to that love, but we can never make Him stop loving us. The quotation of Psalm 44:22 in verse 36 is an Old Testament description of how Paul sees the Christian life: daily slaughter. We can read about the slaughter of Christians in the first few centuries of the church's history and marvel at the confidence with which those believers faced pain and death. Paul claims simply that none of that is enough to convince him that God doesn't love him; and if God loves him, who or what can ultimately hurt him? "No, in all these things we are more than conquerors through him who loved us" (Romans 8:37).

Paul brings the whole line of thought to a climax by challenging all the mysteries of creation. He has already established the fact that human powers can't ultimately triumph over God's beloved. Now he takes in all the extra-terrestrial powers, real or imaginary, which caused fear among his contemporaries. "For I am convinced that neither death nor life [over which we have no ultimate control even with all the discoveries of modern science], neither angels nor demons [which are obviously out of our control], neither the present nor the future [since time is the context in which we live and not of our own contrivance], nor any powers [those spiritual powers that (see 1 Corinthians 15:24-26) will finally be destroyed in the end-time], neither height nor depth [he is likely referring here to terms of astrology], nor anything else in all creation, will be able to separate us from the love of God that is in Christ Jesus our Lord" (Romans 8:38, 39).

It is hard to imagine how Paul could have listed any more terms that would have struck such fear into the hearts of people of his day. Each age of history seems to develop its own phobias, as has ours; but we can live in the assurance that the love of God is unconquerable. There is nothing we or anybody else can do to make God stop loving us. In fact, because of that love, we can be assured that all things, even the bad things, are ultimately working together for good. Thank God!

CHAPTER TEN

Israel and the Gospel

Romans 9:1—11:36

Students of the Bible have long noticed that chapters 9, 10, and 11 seem not to be so closely connected to the train of thought of the epistle to the Romans as do the other chapters. It has been suggested that this section might be a sermon or essay written by the apostle for some other occasion and inserted here for personal reasons. However, a closer look at the epistle shows several questions brought up in Romans 3:1-20 and other questions to which those would lead the concerned Christian that have not yet been fully dealt with. Furthermore, if, as we are suggesting, Paul is aiming his epistle to a serious misunderstanding between Jews and Gentiles in the Roman Christian community, then an extended discussion of Israel in the plan of God is quite relevant. It is not only important for the Jewish Christians to understand their own status and the status of their unbelieving kin, but also vital for the Gentiles in the church to see more clearly the divine strategy so as to be able to appreciate their Jewish brothers and sisters.

So whether or not these three chapters were originally prepared independent of the epistle, they deal with questions integral to the theme and purpose of the whole epistle and obviously personally important to the author. He introduces the discussion with an intense statement of his personal concern for his people (Romans 9:1-5). He then discusses the sovereignty of God (Romans 9:6-29), the history of God's redeeming activities (Romans 9:30—10:21), and the hope of Israel, which touches the hope of every Christian (Romans 11:1-32). The passage closes with a stirring doxology (Romans 11:33-36). We'll look at each of these in order.

Paul's Personal Introduction (9:1-5)

The apostle begins this section with an intense statement, which he opens with a sort of oath: "I speak the truth in Christ—I am not lying, my conscience confirms it in the Holy Spirit" (Romans 9:1). This triple claim to sincerity in what he is about to say is uncharacteristic of Paul and so draws the reader's attention to the importance of what is about to be stated.

Not only is he determined to have us believe what he is saying, but he is also willing to reveal his deepest feelings about the subject, his "great sorrow and unceasing anguish in [his] heart" (Romans 9:2). His intense sorrow is for his "brothers ... the people of Israel," for whose sake Paul said he wished he could be "cursed and cut off from Christ" if it would bring their salvation. In the light of his opening statement, we can hardly dismiss this as hyperbole. We can only step back and wonder at the depth of the love of this former Pharisee. He stands in the lineage of Moses and a number of the prophets who expressed to God their willingness to die for the salvation of their people. (See Exodus 32:31, 32.)

In Romans 3:1, Paul had put the question, "What advantage, then, is there in being a Jew?" In the next verse, he answered himself, "Much in every way! First of all, they have been entrusted with the very words of God." But we seek in vain in chapter 3 for any other examples of the "much in every way." Now, in Romans 9:4, 5, Paul offers some more advantages of Jewishness: "Theirs is the adoption as sons; theirs the divine glory, the covenants, the receiving of the law, the temple worship and the promises. Theirs are the patriarchs, and from them is traced the human ancestry of Christ, who is God over all, forever praised! Amen." The opening phrase of verse 4 I have connected to verse 3, but actually *the people of Israel* connects the two statements. Israel was and remains the name that is held in great respect by the descendants of Jacob. This is, of course, the name given to the modern nation created in 1948 for these people. One advantage of being a Jew is simply the privilege of bearing the name *Israel*. Their special relationship to God is spotlighted by the word *adoption*. Hosea 11 is not the only Old Testament passage that deals with this relationship, but it is one of the most moving, when one hears God say, "Out of Egypt I called my son."

We have already discussed the use of the term *glory* in chapters 1, 3, 5, and 8. In those passages, *glory* referred to an element of the intent of the Creator for all of humanity; but here it refers to a special portion of the glory (the presence of God) with which Israel was graced. (See Exodus 24:15-20 and 33:12—34:35.)

The plural form *covenants* seems strange to us, accustomed as we are to referring to *the* Mosaic Covenant. The fact that a number of old manuscripts change it to the singular indicates that others have also been caught off guard by it. But the Old Testament does refer to several covenants (Genesis 15, Exodus 19, Deuteronomy 29, Joshua 8, and 2 Samuel 23, for instance), and they all go to comprise the riches of Israel. The outstanding covenant, of course, is the one given through Moses accompanied by legislation. As troublesome as the law might seem to others, the dedicated Jew (not excluding the messianic Jew) considered it one of God's finest gifts. Part of that law deals with the rites of worship of Israel, primarily (but not exclusively) temple rites. Such gifts, when accompanied by the multitude of promises of God, surely comprise a treasure store of advantages for the Israelite.

But Paul is not yet finished. Two more elements of Israel's treasure must be mentioned. First, the patriarchs. This term is often used to refer not only to Abraham, Isaac, Jacob, and the twelve sons of Jacob, but also to David. (See Acts 2:29.) Thus, Paul has in mind the whole history of God's special people through whom He has prepared His greatest blessing, the Christ. In this context, we should remember that the term *Christ* is not a name, but a title. It is the Greek equivalent of the Hebrew word *Messiah*. The Christ is the fulfillment of those promises to which Paul has alluded: He has fulfilled the sacrificial worship rites, He will be shown to be the "end of the law" (Romans 10:4), He is the bringer of a new covenant, He opens the glory to everybody, and He makes possible the adoption of every believer. His human descent is through the Israelites, but actually He is "over all." The final statement/doxology of this verse is hard to "rightly divide." The major question is whether or not Paul is actually calling the Christ God. We have plenty of reasons to expect that he could make the claim of the divinity of Christ, but he nowhere else explicitly calls Christ God. The most natural way to translate the statement, following its word order in the original, is, "From whom is the Christ according to the flesh, who is over all, God be praised forever. Amen." The lordship of Christ "over all" is clearly stated; but we should probably not insist that Paul indicate that Christ is also above God. It is more natural to understand him to be saying that the Christ is the Sovereign of the creation and to give praise to God for that greatest of all of His gifts.

The Sovereignty of God (9:6-29)

This passage shows clearly that the twentieth century was not the first to hear the false alternatives: either God is not powerful enough to right the wrongs of human experience or He is unwilling to do so and is, therefore, unjust. Paul here attacks these false alternatives by showing first (verses 6-13) that the plight of the Jews—God's chosen people who have rejected their Savior—is not the fault of the weakness of God or of His word and by showing second (verses 14-29) that it is absurd for finite human beings to accuse the one who is the very definition of justice or righteousness of being unjust. Paul recognized the importance for the Christian, no matter what his or her racial or national background may be, to submit to the God who was, who is, and who will be the sovereign Lord of the universe that He has created.

Paul has already faced the reality of his people's rejection of the one sent as their Messiah and Savior. He has confessed his personal grief at this reality and the lengths he is willing to go to rectify it. He has shown the great advantages that belong to Israel, which should have prepared them to recognize and receive the Christ. The question that now must be raised is why? This question is always ultimately a theological question. Why is God doing this? Why did God permit this to happen? These are the questions Paul faces with his opening statement, "It is not as though God's word had failed" (Romans 9:6). The infallibility of the promises of God is a vital element of the faith of the Christian. We have already noted this in the experience of Abraham, to which Paul has called our attention in chapter 4. Paul, in Romans 4:20, 21, describes the faith of Abraham in terms of "being fully persuaded that God had power to do what he had promised." This faith of Abraham, which was supported by the subsequent history of his people and reiterated by the prophets, is the basis of the Christian faith, also. Paul wisely sees that this infallibility must be upheld if we are to have any security in our relationship with God through Christ.

To make his point, Paul offers two propositions. "For not all who are descended from Israel are Israel. Nor because they are his descendants are they all Abraham's children" (Romans 9:6, 7). He deals with these two statements in reverse order, looking into the matter of descent from Abraham in verses 7-9 and the relationship with Israel (Jacob) in verses 10-13.

Paul's first piece of evidence is God's decision that only "through Isaac" would Abraham's "offspring . . . be reckoned." So even in the Hebrew Bible (Paul's statement is a quotation from Genesis 21:12), God is quoted as recognizing only certain of Abraham's descendants as offspring of the promise. Paul's explanation is that "it is not the natural children who are God's children, but it is the children of the promise who are regarded as Abraham's offspring." Thus, Paul shifts the discussion to the basics: the will of God. He sees that it does no good in a discussion of why things have happened as they have to leave God out of the picture, unless one is an atheist. He does not hesitate to tackle the hard issues, and his example should remind us that our tendency to duck or side-step such questions stems from a lack of faith and results in the loss of confidence in us and in our God on the part of the people with whom we have to do. When all the other factors are dealt with in any human event, if we have not dealt with God's will and power, we are not yet finished. "Children of the promise" are persons who have been brought into a special relationship with God by God's own choice. It was not just any son of Abraham whose descendants would be the chosen people; it was the son of God's choice. God chooses whom He will. If one is chosen, it is by God's grace and by nothing else.

Romans 9:10-13 picks up the theme of verse 6 with its reference to Israel. Those two propositions parallel each other, really making the same point, but using two separate historical points of reference. The earlier passage centered on Isaac as the son of the promise; here, the reference is to Isaac's own children. Once again, but this time with an even more radical reference, pointing out the complete innocence of both Jacob and Esau, Paul draws our attention to God's decision as the determining factor in the history of salvation through the Israelites. On the human level, this does not seem fair. On the human level, such favoritism is not fair. But we must recall that Paul has moved this whole discussion off the human level and onto the divine. We are talking about God here—the Creator and Sustainer of the universe—not just another parent. God's understanding and wisdom are infinite. So what is unfair is our insistence on judging God's will and acts as we would judge those of our fellow human beings. The most radical statement of God's sovereignty is here: "Jacob I loved, but Esau I hated" (Romans 9:13; cf. Malachi 1:2, 3). If we are to question

God's justice, we must be faced with the most radical questions available.

This concern is obviously not an invention of the modern age; Paul sees fit to approach it directly in verses 14-18. "Is God unjust? Not at all! For he says to Moses, 'I will have mercy on whom I have mercy, and I will have compassion on whom I have compassion'" (Romans 9:14, 15). We have already noted (see chapter 6) Paul's characteristic use of questions that he answers with his strong negative. That's what we have here. He does not hesitate to deal with such a basic theological question, and he cannot leave it unanswered for long. So he continues his argument for God's sovereignty, turning now from the patriarchs to the lawgiver. For the Jewish side of his readership, it is important that he deal with a law text (Exodus 33:19), since texts from the law documents were often used to indicate that God's choice was somehow dependent on the righteousness of the human being. Quite to the contrary, argues Paul: "It does not, therefore, depend on man's desire or effort, but on God's mercy" (Romans 9:16). Here, for the first time, Paul uses a qualitative term for God's will. He first had to establish the fact that God has the right to decide independent of our concepts of justice, but now he can afford to point out that God's choices, in fact, are not arbitrary, but are based on His mercy (the Hebrew equivalent of grace).

Again, in verse 17, Paul turns to a Scripture quotation. Since the basic question concerns the reliability of the Word of God, such quotations are determinative. "For the Scripture says to Pharaoh: 'I raised you up for this very purpose, that I might display my power in you and that my name might be proclaimed in all the earth.'" Whether or not the modern reader is satisfied that Paul takes care of all our problems in relation to the sovereignty of God, we must admit that he brings up both the most radical questions and the most difficult texts. The history of the exodus and the conquest of Canaan raises serious questions because of the slaughter of seemingly innocent people at the command of God. So Paul goes right to the heart of the matter, reminding his readers that the book of Exodus indicates that God made it impossible for Pharaoh to do any other than he did (Exodus 9:16) so as to display God's power. Without softening the situation or attempting a detailed explanation (which, even if it were possible, is beside the point here), he merely reiterates the fact that "God has mercy on whom he wants to have mercy, and he hardens whom he wants to harden" (Romans 9:18). If God has the power and the right to do the positive, He can also do the negative.

Now that Paul has dealt with the underlying theological quandaries caused by the rejection of the Messiah by his own race, he can turn to more individual questions. He did the former with reference to the patriarchs and Moses in the beginnings of the nation of Israel; he will now refer to the rest of Scripture: the wisdom literature and the prophets.

Romans 9:19 begins another section of diatribe, similar to that in chapter 6. This series of questions and answers begins with the double question: "Then why does God still blame us? For who resists his will?" The problem of God's justice has not yet been settled. If everything that happens is caused by God, why should somebody else be held responsible for anything? There is no simple answer to this question, but it should help us to pay attention to the way Paul deals with it. First, he presents some statements from Isaiah and the apocryphal book, the Wisdom of Solomon. Paul's purpose here is obviously not to answer all the readers' questions, but to direct our loyalty and obedience to God. It is absurd for us to question the justice of the one who is the source of the concept of justice. It would have been just as clear to Paul as it is to us that human beings are not inanimate, unthinking pottery, but his focus is on God, whose intelligence and power are as far beyond ours as are the intelligence and power of the potter above that of the pot. The believer must admit that the Creator has "the right" to do whatever He wills.

In verses 22-29, Paul begins to put some of these thoughts together. He picks up his reference both to the wrath of God from chapter 1 and to the mercy of God, which he has alluded to earlier in this chapter; and he does this to push forward into a discussion of God's ultimate strategy in history. The "what if" approach indicates again that Paul is staying in his argumentation mode and not making arrogant statements about God. He does not pretend to have pat answers to all the mysteries of the universe, but he does know God. He describes here just one hypothetical possible explanation for God's permitting or engineering both good and evil to exist side by side in human history. What Paul is convinced of is that God in His mercy has chosen to call into his family not only Jews but also Gentiles, a conviction that the epistle has mentioned a number of times, beginning in chapter 1. The point again is simply that God is in charge, and it is absurd for His creatures to question His decisions.

The section is brought to a conclusion by a string of Old Testament quotations from Hosea and Isaiah. Paul does not comment directly on these passages. He has already made his argument for the right of God to decide for or against human beings. All he needs to do now is add some more authority to his point by quotations from the prophets. He has used samples of all the major divisions of his Scripture to undergird his point that God is in charge.

The History of God's Redeeming Activities (9:30—10:21)

Romans 9:30 introduces this section with a device Paul has used before. (See Romans 6:1; 7:7; 8:31.) "What then shall we say?" Thus, he begins dealing with the implications of his argument and at the same time drawing his readers into the process. His conclusion is stated in two propositions, connected by a question. (See Romans 9:30-32.)

So Paul thus summarizes his contention and sets the stage for what he must deal with now: the meaning of God's redeeming activities in history. The reference to the stone of stumbling is found in Isaiah 8:14 and 28:16, which Paul quotes in Romans 9:33. By bringing the two passages together in this way, he shows both the negative and the positive results expected in the coming of the Messiah. Although Paul never shrinks from the negative aspects of the gospel, he consistently balances such references with the positive—that aspect to which he had personally testified in Romans 1:16, "I am not ashamed of the gospel."

Chapter 10 opens in much the same way as chapter 9, with a personal statement of the author's concern for his people and statements that describe both the positive and negative aspects of those people. His "heart's desire and prayer" for Israel is for their salvation. "They are zealous for God, but their zeal is not based on knowledge" (Romans 10:1, 2). Paul certainly knows what he is talking about here. He can be seen as the model of Jewish zeal without knowledge in his pre-Christian life. His zeal for God drove him to lead a persecution of those he saw as disobedient heretics—the Christians. At that time, he understood righteousness as something that the person does instead of something the person receives from God. The person who so understands the nature of righteousness is therefore not able to submit to God's righteousness because he/she is too busy trying to become righteous (Romans 10:3).

But Christ changes all that: "Christ is the end of the law so that there may be righteousness for everyone who believes" (Romans 10:4). The original language version of this sentence is very simple—so simple that a translator must add several words to make it understandable in any other language. The major difficulty is how *righteousness* functions in the sentence. The NIV version, cited above, connects it with the end of the sentence: "for everyone who believes," and thus makes it a description of the results of Christ's being the end of the law. But it could just as well (and I think even better) connect to the former part of the sentence, explaining how Paul understands the scope of the term *end*. He would then be saying, "Christ is the end of the law as a means to righteousness." He certainly does not want to leave the impression that Christ means that the law or the Old Testament is no longer necessary. If that were his meaning, he would hardly have written this section with so many citations of those Scriptures. It is more likely that he sees Christ as having fulfilled the law's purpose by obeying its spirit perfectly and by dying at its instigation, so to speak, in order to make it possible for the sinner to receive righteousness by the grace of God.

The next nine verses (Romans 10:5-13) explain the contrast even more fully. Here, Paul graphically—and with much quoting from Deuteronomy, Isaiah, and Joel—shows that legal righteousness depends upon the person's perfect obedience, which leaves all of us out, while God's righteousness in Christ is available to the believer by means of the confession of faith.

Paul introduces this topic with another passage that is very difficult to understand (verses 5-10). The sentence structure is exceedingly complex, with quotations from Deuteronomy 30 interrupted several times by short explanations as it moves the reader with hardly a breath into the Christian confession. But it seems to me that in this context, which is heavily dedicated to concern for Israel, Paul is in a sense putting himself in the place of Moses, whose words he quotes. Moses was giving his last advice to the people before they crossed into Canaan, warning them not to seek God anywhere other than in the word from Him that was already theirs. Paul implies that the legalistic righteousness is tantamount to trying to find or win something that the people of God already had. A further implication is that the Christian who tries to win his or her own salvation is ignoring the significance of both the incarnation and the resurrection. Christ has already come from Heaven and has already risen from the dead. Any attempt to earn the gift He has already given to us is, at best, foolish and, at worst, idolatrous.

In verses 11-13 Paul completes this point by quoting two prophets, Isaiah 28:16 and Joel 2:32, and by stating the universal consequences of the gospel: "there is no difference between Jew and Gentile." Once again, Paul in one statement both shows the implications of his argument and points to another theme that he must deal with more fully—that of the relationship of Jew and Gentile in the kingdom.

But first, he must complete another line of thought, which commands this passage and which is highlighted by the Joel quotation—the means of evangelism. Joel has promised salvation to "everyone who calls on the name of the Lord." Paul follows this up with a series of questions that leads the reader to a consideration of the place of preaching and the preacher in the plan of God (Romans 10:14, 15a). The logic here seems so obvious that it is amazing how often we ignore it. Throughout its history, the church has produced thinkers and leaders who have become so enamored of one or another truth of the gospel that they tend to neglect other truths. So some say, "Faith alone" is the means of salvation. Others say, "Grace alone." Others stand for baptism or church activities or good living. Paul's series of questions should remind us that no one aspect of the plan of salvation stands alone. He has already established that it all depends for its efficacy on the death and resurrection of Christ (see Romans 4:25), which is the greatest gift of God's grace. Now he has claimed that "it is with your mouth that you confess and are saved." Here he shows how confession is dependent on faith, and faith is dependent on hearing, and hearing is dependent on speaking, and speaking in this case is dependent on being commissioned. Faith is not some miraculous gift; it is the response of the thinking person to what that person hears. The message does not come in a voice from the clouds, it is borne by a human messenger. And that messenger does not dream up the message on his or her own, but is given it and is sent by its giver. It is all from God, but it is all by means of human beings. Verse 15 closes with the stirring description from Isaiah 52:7, "How beautiful on the mountains are the feet of those who bring good news!"

That, of course, poses a problem. If it is possible for any person to hear and believe to be saved, why do some who hear refuse to believe? Why is it that "not all the Israelites accepted the good news"? (See Romans 10:16.) The quotation of Isaiah 53:1 shows that the problem is not new even in Paul's age. One could wish that Paul's answer were clearer. Verse 17 is often quoted but rarely explained: "Consequently, faith comes from hearing the message, and the message is heard through the word of Christ." The more I study this verse, the clearer it becomes to me that I don't understand much of it. We should note that the term *message* does not appear in the original. Thus, even though Paul is assuming that if something is heard, it is something understandable and thus is a message, his emphasis seems to be more on the process of hearing than on the message, at least in this verse. Let us not forget that at the heart of the Jewish faith then and now lies a call known as the *Shema*—a call that begins, "Hear, Oh Israel." Let us remember also that Paul's own experience on the road to Damascus consisted of a conversation in which he heard the risen Christ. And let us keep in mind that Paul had already written to the Corinthians, "For since in the wisdom of God the world through its wisdom did not know him, God was pleased through the foolishness of what was preached to save those who believe" (1 Corinthians 1:21). Even in this verse, the original term that is translated "what was preached" is only the single word *kerygma,* which is always understood as an orally delivered message. It could be that we Christians who are engulfed in printed and recorded words need extra reminders of the place of oral presentations in ancient cultures and the continuing importance of preaching in the history of the church.

The kind of hearing that becomes the soil out of which faith grows must be hearing in the Jewish sense, that is, paying attention with the determination to obey the word recognized as coming from God. That kind of hearing will recognize the voice of Christ in the truth heard from God. As Paul describes this process, he does not indicate that this production of faith is dependent on the gullibility of the listeners nor on the persuasiveness of the preacher, but that Christ himself is involved. The word of Christ is the decisive factor in this process. The way Paul puts this, it is impossible to take him as meaning a message about Christ. He is using a term that refers to a unit of expression and not to a general message. Thus, effective preaching/hearing

119

depends upon the clarity and faithfulness of the preacher, the willingness of the audience to pay attention and take the message to heart, and the active participation of Christ himself. We can assume that Christ is present where the gospel is being communicated (see Matthew 28:20); so the effectiveness of the preaching of the gospel depends on the faithfulness of us who preach it and the consecrated attention of us who listen to it.

Paul has two remaining questions relating to this topic: "Did they not hear?" and, "Did Israel not understand?" In verses 18-21, he addresses these two questions by presenting a series of quotations from all three of the major divisions of the Old Testament. Psalm 19 is an interesting place to begin, since its first half is a poetic description of the universal proclamation of the greatness of God by means of the physical creation, and its second half deals with the word of the law of God. Israel has heard, in the sense of being exposed to the revelation. But have they really paid attention? Deuteronomy 32:21 sets up an argument that Paul will develop in chapter 11, indicating that God is even somehow at work in Israel's rejecting of their Messiah. And then the words from Isaiah 65 make clear that Israel has not understood because they are "a disobedient and obstinate people" (Romans 10:21).

This chapter's description of the process of God's redemptive activities in history ends, thus, with a strong indictment of people to whom the will of God was revealed clearly but who refused to accept it. It would be too easy for us to point the finger at the Jews now, but Paul makes it clear in the next chapter that we have no right to do that. We should rather check ourselves to be sure that when we gather to hear the word preached, we listen intently with fresh minds and hearts and wills ready to do what we recognize as the word of Christ. Let's not stop praying for our preachers, but let's also prepare ourselves to be good hearers of the word, ready to translate our hearing into doing.

The Hope of Israel (11:1-36)

There are two questions about Israel that Paul must face. The first is in Romans 11:1, "Did God reject his people?" He has faced the fact that Israel (God's people) rejected God's Messiah. Does this force God to reject them? "By no means!" Once again, we are reminded that God does not follow the same paths of thinking and acting as do sinful human beings. One of the major themes of the Old Testament is the faithfulness of God even in situations of human unfaithfulness. Paul maintains that faith here. He offers as evidence first of all himself: an Israelite of the tribe of Benjamin. He could as easily have mentioned hundreds of other Israelites who had become Christians. So it is obvious that God had not rejected His people in general.

Then Paul points to this group of Jewish believers as another example of the remnant pointed out so often in the Old Testament (Romans 11:2-6). Thus, both present reality and historical precedent offer themselves as evidence of God's continuing activity on behalf of His chosen people.

Paul's contention is that the favor of God has always been both universal (since His intent has been to redeem all humanity) and faith-specific (since individuals have always been able to reject His call, and they have rejected it). That is where he concludes his answer to this question: "What then? What Israel sought so earnestly it did not obtain, but the elect did. The others were hardened" (Romans 11:7). Here he offers three Old Testament passages: Deuteronomy 29:4; Isaiah 29:10; and Psalm 69:22, 23. Again, we are face to face with the issue of human responsibility and divine sovereignty—a problem that we have already noted is not to be solved in a neat and logical way. We must leave it just where Paul does: some have refused to believe (Romans 10:21) and thus display that God has hardened them (how we are not told).

Paul's second and final question in this chapter appears in verse 11: "Again I ask: Did they stumble so as to fall beyond recovery? Not at all!" Here we face a double question: is there any meaning in Israel's failure, and is there any hope remaining for Israel? The answer comes quickly, since Paul does not see the need any longer for extended argumentation. "Rather, because of their transgression, salvation has come to the Gentiles to make Israel envious. But if their transgression means riches for the world, and their loss means riches for the Gentiles, how much greater riches will their fullness bring!" (Romans 11:11, 12). This double contention commands the rest of the chapter. Paul is convinced that God is using Israel's rejection of her Messiah to bring salvation to the Gentiles and that the jealousy this will arouse in the Israelites will attract them eventually to the gospel. He has seen the former of these convictions work in situations where his preaching of the gospel was rejected by a synagogue but was welcomed in Gentile society. The second of his contentions, although he probably saw it work in a few individual cases, remained and remains today a matter of hope. Faith in the God whose word never fails demands the hope that eventually that word will be heard by all people, especially by the chosen people.

In verses 13-16, Paul reiterates these two convictions, using different metaphors. At first glance, verse 16 seems not to fit; but as we consider the whole context, we see that Paul is restating his jealousy point in verses 13-15, and then, in verse 16, he reminds us of the fact with which he began this chapter, that a number of Israelites have become Christians and that they work a blessing on the rest of the race. Thus, once again, we have two arguments for hope for God's chosen people.

Verses 17-24 focus on the analogy of the olive tree and its branches. As we look at the details of this discussion, it becomes obvious that Paul is not giving a botany lesson here, but is rather looking realistically at the position of the Gentile Christians. He has indicated in verse 13 that he is speaking to Gentiles here, not Jews. They are the branches "grafted in among the others." As such, they have no room for boasting. They ought rather to take heed that they not fall into disbelief. "Do not be arrogant, but be afraid. For if God did not spare the natural branches, he will not spare you either" (Romans 11:20, 21). Such arrogance as he is warning against here is a subtle but powerful temptation. It lies at the base of too many acts of prejudice in the years since Paul wrote the warning. Anti-semitism, or any racist attitude, has too often found nourishment in the belief that God has somehow rejected certain people. Paul reminds us once again of the major contention of the whole epistle: salvation is a gift of God's grace, which we receive by faith and which we reject by a lack of faith. Each individual enters this relationship with God on this same basis; so there is no room for arrogance or feelings of racial or individual superiority. There is room only for the deep respect for God that he labels "fear."

But he hastens to make it clear that God is not to be feared because He is capricious. God can be trusted. There is eternal security in God. He treats each person fairly and like every other person. But there is great insecurity in sinful human beings. We can be solid believers one day and extreme doubters the next. These two facts should be kept in our minds as a pair, so that when we feel insecure in our relationship with God, we recognize that the problem is in us and not in God. There is certainly no place in the Christian life for arrogance, nor should there be a hint of mistrust in the faithfulness of God. It is up to the Christian, then, to praise God for His faithfulness and to exercise continuously one's faith faculties. Only in this way can we be sure of continuing in the role of branches in the Lord's tree.

In verses 25-32, Paul summarizes what he has been saying here, and he does it under the heading, "I do not want you to be ignorant of this mystery, brothers, so that you may not be conceited." The term *mystery,* as becomes even clearer in Ephesians 3, could as well be translated "strategy." God has been working out His purpose on the stage of human history, and He has revealed to human beings from time to time small pieces of that mystery/ strategy. Here, Paul is revealing his part: "Israel has experienced a hardening in part until the full number of the Gentiles has come in. And so all Israel will be saved" (Romans 11:25, 26). He has already made it clear that this hardening is the result of Israel's unbelief. Now he points out again that God is using it for a time to let the Gentiles enter the kingdom. He gives us no indication of how long that time will be or of how many Gentiles he means by "the full number." We need only understand that God is still in charge, and that, therefore, we can be sure that His chosen people will be saved. We could argue for a lifetime about what Paul means by "all Israel," but the point is that there is hope for mass obedience on the part of God's chosen people, because God is working out His strategy. The promises in Isaiah 59:20, 21 and 27:9, which Paul quotes here, are too explicit and pointed to ignore. And they drive Paul to reiterate in even more explicit and general terms than he has used previously what he has been saying.

> As far as the gospel is concerned, they are enemies on your account; but as far as election is concerned, they are loved on account of the patriarchs, for God's gifts and his call are irrevocable. Just as you who were at one time disobedient to God have now received mercy as a result of their disobedience, so they too have now become disobedient in order that they too may now receive mercy as a result of God's mercy to you. For God has bound all men over to disobedience so that he may have mercy on them all (Romans 11:28-32).

How can this last extreme but clear statement be reconciled with any human logic? Apparently, it can't. It seems to be beyond

Paul's ability either to understand or to explain. All we can do is consider the greatness and faithfulness of God and, as does Paul here, break into adoration. Verse 33 is a typical Pauline doxology (compare Ephesians 3:20, 21). "Oh, the depth of the riches of the wisdom and knowledge of God! How unsearchable his judgments, and his paths beyond tracing out!" The person who thinks about his or her faith, as all believers should, comes periodically to a place where human understanding bumps against a barrier. We cannot hope to understand God completely, since then He would be no greater than we are. At times, we must stop thinking and begin worshiping. Paul continues his worship by quoting (in verses 34 and 35) Isaiah and Job, both of whom had experienced this same limitation. Again we could ask, who has ever tried to reason out the ways of the Creator who cannot empathize with these great thinkers? "For from him and through him and to him are all things. To him be the glory forever! Amen" (Romans 11:36).

This final line of this section of the epistle is, as happens so often in Paul's writings, a doxology—a statement of praise to God. But even in moments of exaltation, such as this one, Paul is obviously still careful of how he states things. When his soul soars, his mind is still involved. There is at least one other similar statement of praise to a pagan deity that stands in the meditations of the Stoic emperor, Marcus Aurelius. There, the pantheistic mystic praises "nature" in the words, "from you are all things, in you are all things, unto you are all things." But the object of Paul's faith is neither part of the creation nor the container of creation, but the Creator, who is a person in His own right, standing outside His creation. All things are from Him; all things have come into being by His command; and all things are heading toward Him as their climax; but the creation is not *in* Him. It is not nature, but nature's God whom we praise. It is not nature's power, but the Lord who has power over nature whom we worship. It is not our environment, but our Creator whom we revere. As is true with everything, the glory is His. When we glorify Him, we give Him but His own; and we creatures discover our true humanity when we say from the heart, "To him be glory forever! Amen."

CHAPTER ELEVEN

Life Shaped by the Gospel

Romans 12:1—13:14

It was the practice of the apostle Paul to lay a foundation of the reality of God's justification and then to build the ethical super-structure of his message to Christians on that solid foundation. The great reformer, Martin Luther, put it this way, "For being comes before doing, but being-acted-upon comes even before being."[29] One of Paul's outstanding transitions from being to doing—from doctrine to ethics—lies before us now. He has already shown the individual Christian as justified by God, through the forgiveness of sin, the redemption from the slavery to sin, the new creation in the participation in Christ's resurrection, and the new life-giving power in the Holy Spirit. He has also answered the theological and historical questions raised by Israel's rejection of the gospel of their Messiah. He can now turn to some practical ethical considerations for the Christian—especially one living in the capital of the empire.

The *therefore* of Romans 12:1 refers back to all that Paul has already written in this letter. We who take such small bites as we work our way through the banquet of the epistle find it hard to remember that the sixteen chapters would have been read all at once by the people who received it, since they would not have needed all the help with language, history, and customs that we need more than 1900 years later. For this reason, I urged the reader to read straight through the book before beginning a detailed study. This would be a good time to read again the first eleven chapters, so as to have in mind the whole tendency of the

---

[29]Martin Luther, *Lectures on Romans,* edited and translated by Wilhelm Pauck (Philadelphia: Westminster Press, 1961), p. 321.

apostle's thought. Only in this way can we appreciate the impact of his *therefore.* He sums it up himself in the statement, "In view of God's mercy." The term *mercy* did not appear in the first eight chapters, but Paul used it several times in chapters 9—11, since it is the Hebrew equivalent of the concept of *grace,* which is dominant in the earlier part of the letter.

The heart of verse 1 is the infinitive clause that is the object of Paul's urging: "to offer your bodies as living sacrifices." Paul uses sacrificial terminology to emphasize the depth of commitment that should follow on God's gracious act of justification. Beyond that, a living sacrifice (as contrasted with a blood sacrifice) indicates that our offering includes in its meaning "to put at God's disposal." The word is used in this way in Romans 6:13, 19; 2 Corinthians 4:14; 11:2; Colossians 1:22, 28; and Ephesians 5:27. That which is to be sacrificed and put at God's disposal is our bodies. To the person who is accustomed to thinking of the church or religion as something primarily concerned with the "soul," it might come as a shock that it is the body that Paul says we are to make the central concern of our worship. He can say that at this point because he has shown clearly how sin has caused the degrading of the human body and its created functions (Romans 1:18-32 and chapter 7), which leads him to identify sin with the human body (Romans 6:6, 12; 7:24); he has proclaimed clearly that God has won His battle for the salvation of humankind in the body of Jesus (Romans 7:4); and He has promised that this salvation will mean a glorification of the body (Romans 8:10-13, 23). So it is these bodies that Paul says should be presented to God—these human persons, these creatures of God. The presentation can be made without hesitation, since God has recreated us in Christ. And just this presentation to God of His own creations is what Paul insists is the Christians' "spiritual worship."

The way Paul states this exhortation indicates that he sees a real contrast between the Christian and the non-Christian. It would be poor English style to translate his words in their original order, since the possessive pronoun *(your)* is the last word in the sentence. But the reader should get the picture Paul had in his mind that "spiritual worship" experiences were available all around the citizen of first-century Rome. These Christians did not live in a religious vacuum; rather their culture was full of religions of all kinds, from the very material pagan idol worship to the extremely mystical and intellectual philosophies. But the Christian gospel and the faith it elicits contrast with other religious experiences by calling for a total human commitment to the Creator of the whole of reality. Such a realization is still important, since our culture is also filled with many kinds of spiritual/intellectual experiences, and since none of these options offers access to the true God or demands total involvement with that God. Only when we Christians understand who we are as redeemed sinners and respond logically by offering our whole selves to God can we either understand or follow fully the advice Paul proceeds to give on the basis of "the mercies of God."

Such correct self-understanding is what Paul himself points to next (Romans 12:3). "Sober judgment" about oneself is difficult but important. Paul obviously saw that the primary problem in this regard for these original readers was overestimation. They must have thought they were being blessed by God because they were worthy of such a blessing or because they had somehow earned it. This was and is not a problem belonging just to Israelites. For such egocentric people, Paul's reprimand is to remember that whatever they are is a gift of God and should be assessed with the mind and in faith. It seems to me that such a reprimand should be heard also by those of us who think of ourselves more lowly than we ought to think. Most churches I have known are mostly populated by people who have never taken seriously the new creation and who, therefore, see themselves as sinners with little worth and no abilities. These people need also to hear that the time of depending on ourselves is past, because of what God has done and is doing through Christ Jesus. As Romans 12:4-8 states, God has given His church the ability to carry out His will in our communities. We should, therefore, be willing to be put to work in the church and to respect the gifts that all other members bring to that body.

Paul did not need to look very far to find an analogy for explaining how a Christian is to understand him- or herself. The body is an ideal picture of how persons should relate to one another in a close-knit community. Paul did not originate this use, but he had earlier written something similar in 1 Corinthians 6:15 and 12:27. Here in Romans 12, he does not identify the church as the body of Christ, as he does in 1 Corinthians, but he places the whole picture "in Christ." His purpose here is not to define the church as a divinely commissioned agent of God's will, but to describe how each believer is to relate to other believers.

127

Once again, Paul's main emphasis is on a simple statement of fact: "We who are many form one body" (Romans 12:5). Since this is true for us because we are "in Christ," the reality is not dependent on our wills or moods. That is just the way it is. Then Paul's second affirmation enriches our understanding: "We have different gifts, according to the grace given us" (Romans 12:6). God brings us into Christ, thus making us individual members of one body, and God gives us specific abilities. That is Paul's description of the reality of the church. Now he is ready to proceed with advice on what to do about it.

The list of gifts in Romans 12:6-8 is representative. Paul offers other lists (sometimes referred to as catalogs) of gifts in 1 Corinthians 12—14 and Ephesians 4, but each list is unique. It appears that there is no authoritative listing of God's gifts, but that rather He gives to each community of believers the gifts they need to do His will in their situation. In the present list, we find three gifts that appear to take special talents (prophesying, teaching, and leadership, the last of which could be translated "administration") and four (serving, encouraging, contributing, and showing mercy) that nearly everybody can do to some extent. Consider, though, the fact that Paul lists these gifts without distinctions and without any discernable order. If we are to categorize them as I just did, we must upset the order in which Paul mentions them. Our order is apparently not Paul's order, nor presumably God's. There is no innate superiority in any gift of God, nor is there any activity listed here that is somehow innately easy to the human being. One might argue that the kind of self-effacing service, never-ending encouragement, sacrificial giving, and unconditional showing of mercy that Paul is pointing to here are much less common and much more difficult than the activities of public speaking, teaching, and administration that get the spotlight in our culture. Time and again, Paul must remind us in one way or another that the way the Christian evaluates things, activities, and persons is not to be conformed to the criteria of this age.

We should note also the words Paul uses to describe *how* the believer is to carry out the will of God. "In proportion to his faith ... serve ... teach ... encourage ... generously ... diligently ... cheerfully" (Romans 12:6-8). Some tasks just demand to be done, but others could be done in the wrong way. The Christian is given both abilities and responsibilities to do God's will in an appropriate manner. God does not give mercy grudgingly and neither should we. We who are partakers of the Heavenly blessings of God's mercy find it appropriate to relate to one another and to the people around us in the world with the same compassion and generosity that our faith tells us God has showered on us.

One who is familiar with 1 Corinthians 12—14 should not be surprised that Paul would follow a discussion of God's gifts to His people with reference to love (Romans 12:9-13).

This is the beginning of a list of exhortations in short format, similar to the proverbs found in the Old Testament and elsewhere. Most of them would fit on a modern-day bumper sticker. Commentators have tried to find a system in the list, so as to outline it, but without much success. Here in verses 9-13, the statements seem to refer most directly to Christians in relation to other Christians; but verse 14 turns without transition to the Christian's relationship to enemies of the faith: "Bless those who persecute you; bless and do not curse." Then the rest of the chapter seems to switch from references to general conduct to a final exhortation (verses 17-21) about how to conduct oneself in the situation of direct enmity.

If we look carefully at the rhetoric of this section of the epistle, we should be able to see how Paul intended this list to strike us. He has finished teaching his readers what it means to be a Christian; now he is teaching how a Christian is to live in the world. Romans 12:1 and 2 introduces the whole section with the appeal to total dedication to God. Verses 3-8 point to the reality of the unity of God's people and the gifts God gives us for living. Chapters 13—15 deal in some detail with specific problems facing these believers in Rome: how to deal with the government and how to solve disagreements among Christians. And here in Romans 12:9-21, we have this list of very real challenges in the life of any Christian, but we have them without any detail or instructions on how to make decisions about them. Surely, what Paul is doing here is offering a number of bits of rather general advice to show the scope of application of the dedicated life of the Christian. It is obvious that he can't address all issues in great detail; so he makes a representative list and then chooses two situations with which to deal in some detail. He takes up the question of the government in Romans 13:1-7. He then comes back to some more general principles in the rest of chapter 13. And then in Romans 14:1—15:12, he deals with the problem of disunity in the church. It would be impossible to prove that one issue is more important than another; but our own experience indicates that one or another issue becomes vital when it is the one defining our present situation.

This is not to say, of course, that these curt bits of advice are so general as to be of no help to us. On the contrary, if we are facing one of these situations, we should be able to follow the principles and the process of decision making that the apostle gives us in the following chapters and be able to live the life that he so artfully and clearly portrays in this brief list of ethical exhortations. As a matter of fact, the admonitions in verses 11 and 12 are helpful guidance to the Christian in any age and in any circumstance. We are always in danger of losing our zeal; actually most of us experience life as a constant struggle to feel as zealous as we wish. The positive admonition is to keep our spiritual fervor. The original statement here describes one who is aglow or boiling with the Spirit. Then, in order not to leave the impression that the Christian's zeal is all a matter of emotion, Paul adds "serving the Lord." Zeal is basically a matter of motivation, and the Holy Spirit is available to us to aid in this regard; but all motivation must lead to the nitty-gritty service that we present to the Lord by performing for people who need it. There are times when the special glow of the Spirit comes only after we have begun serving. That is to say, there are times when we must get to work even if we don't feel like it; and then we find the glow returning.

Some commentators insist that this whole passage is a series of proverb couplets, but I agree with those who gave us the verse divisions here, that verses 11 and 12 are triplets. As we saw in verse 11, so verse 12 presents a natural progression. To "be joyful in hope," we must have somehow come to terms with living as a Christian in this world. Even though Christians should always have a forward look, we should also be able to find joy in our service in the world. Sometimes that service will bring "affliction," in which circumstance Paul exhorts us to be "patient." The kind of patience the apostle is describing here is endurance. We are not just to sit and take it, but to continue the struggle as an athlete continues the long distance run to the end. And the secret to the Christian's ability to live such a life of victory is to be "faithful in prayer." We dare not underestimate the importance of a disciplined life of prayer for the believer. Without communication with the Father, we cannot expect either the inner resources of the Spirit or the effectiveness in service that are otherwise available to us.

At the end of these rather specific exhortations, Paul gives us another general statement, this one applying at least one aspect of being "transformed" (Romans 12:2). Those who do not allow their environment to determine their life-style, but rather live as persons being transformed by Christ, will "not be overcome by evil, but overcome evil with good." If such a life-style were easy or automatic for Christians, Paul would hardly have had to mention it. Similarly, if it were impossible, he would hardly have exhorted us to do it. The Christian life-style is neither automatic nor impossible, but those who try to live at peace with everyone and who endure even under trying circumstances are going to shine like lights in the world, to the glory of God.

The apostle has depicted in this chapter a community of Christians that has great power. The kind of persons who are totally dedicated to God and transformed to do God's will instead of being molded by the age in which they live (Romans 12:1, 2) are different from their neighbors—they have their own kind of power. But when those same people are united in a community (Romans 12:3-8), their power can, and did, turn the world upside down. When Christians know that they are so united that it can be said of them that "each member belongs to all the others" (Romans 12:5), then they will be able to live the kind of life characterized by Paul's sketch in verses 9-21. Furthermore, this is just the kind of community for which people long in an age of alienation, such as ours. Such a light should not be hidden in a world of darkness.

For this reason, it is important to consider the relationship of the Christian with the society at large. In Rome, that society was dominated by the government; so we should not be surprised that Paul next turns to the Christian's relationship with the government.

The exhortation in Romans 13:1-5 is rather clear, so we hardly need to add any details. It should be noted that, for the Christian, Paul lists two levels of motivation: fear (or common sense) and conscience. Believers are like others in that we don't want to be jailed or otherwise penalized for infractions of the law; so it makes sense to obey the law. Unlike unbelievers, however, we also have a deeper motivation. We recognize the source of all authority to be in God, and so we obey because of an inner compulsion. The Christian's conscience is even more powerful than fear of punishment. This is illustrated dramatically later in the history of the

131

martyr

church by the Christians who were willing to die (often brutally) at the hands of their government rather than renounce their faith in Christ. Such decisions were being made even before the writing of the New Testament books was completed, as is shown in Revelation 13. There the government is described as a beast and a second beast, which make war on the Christians. That and other passages in the New Testament make it clear that the Christian is to be faithful to God when the government is in conflict with that primary loyalty.

For Paul, writing in the early years of Nero's reign as emperor of Rome, there was no obvious conflict. In fact, the power of Rome made possible his travel and correspondence around the empire. It would not be long after the writing of the epistle that Paul would be in a Roman prison, first in Jerusalem, then in Caesarea, then finally in Rome (Acts 21:37—28:31). Even then, Paul's Roman citizenship was an advantage to him, and his being under guard seemed not to be a great hindrance to the spread of the gospel. So then, Paul could without compromise write to the Roman Christians, "This is also why you pay taxes, for the authorities are God's servants, who give their full time to governing. Give everyone what you owe him: If you owe taxes, pay taxes; if revenue, then revenue; if respect, then respect; if honor, then honor" (Romans 13:6, 7). This attitude still makes sense for the Christian who lives under a government that permits people freely to exercise their religious beliefs. We are all expected as far as possible to "live at peace with everyone" (Romans 12:18), but there are many Christians who daily must apply the principle, "We must obey God rather than men" (Acts 5:29).

In the last two paragraphs of chapter 13, Paul returns to a more general mode of exhortation. Verse 5 picks up on the theme of what we owe and leads on to the principle of love, which Paul calls "the fulfillment of the law" (Romans 12:10). Any attempt (and there have been several) to drive a wedge between Paul and Jesus runs aground on this passage. This is so similar to the wording of several different teachings of Jesus found in the gospels that it appears that Paul must have been aware of those teachings. The surprise here is that Paul would quote the Old Testament law at all, after what he wrote in Romans 7:7-13; but we see here that Paul is not out to destroy the law (any more than Jesus was). He is rather teaching that the law was not given as a way to become worthy of salvation, but as a way to live once one has received the salvation available because of God's grace. Christ, he has claimed (Romans 10:4), is the fulfillment of the law; and now he specifies love as the law's fulfillment. He is careful to use two different words for fulfillment, as is shown by the translation of Romans 10:4 as "the end of the law." But the two statements are closely related, the first pointing to Christ as the goal toward which the law was moving, and the second spotlighting love as the ethical principle which fills any and all gaps in the commandments.

At this point, Paul inserts another motivation for Christian living—the one scholars call "eschatology." The warning that the Judgment Day is coming is an important reminder for every Christian in any age. No matter how one thinks about the end time, we all should realize that every day brings us closer to our own end, whether that end is the cataclysmic coming of our Lord or the quiet death of the individual. For the person who believes in the Christ who will judge the living and the dead, it is absurd to be involved in any activity of which we would be ashamed at His appearing. The deeds and the things that belong to an age that is, at best, temporary should never command our primary loyalty. And the deeds and the things that belong to the reign of evil should have no place at all in the life of the Christian. When Augustine read these verses, his tears flowed in repentance for the years wasted in such living, and his life from that time on was the living sacrifice Paul had described (see above, pages 15, 16).

So we see that the dedicated and transformed Christian is expected to do more than enjoy his or her new life in the company of those who share the experience. That new life is to be lived in full view of, and participation in, the world in which we find ourselves—a world of people, some friendly and some mean; a world of authorities, some helpful, some hateful; a world of temptations, both attractive and dangerous. But clothed with Christ, we can live in the world and overcome it.

CHAPTER TWELVE

Relationships That Reflect the Gospel

Romans 14:1—15:13

These thirty-six verses deal in an intense manner with what appears to have been a real problem situation in the church at Rome. The direct form of address (see Romans 14:4) makes it obvious that the author is not giving a generic ethical teaching, but rather knows something about the congregation(s) in Rome. Therefore, this passage deserves careful treatment. It is too often hastily covered in a teacher's eagerness to get finished with a study. Yet, if Paul was aware of tension among the believers in Rome—tension that could easily disunite the church—then this passage was likely a major reason for his writing the epistle. All that he has taught so far in the epistle can be seen as a description of what it means to be a Christian. This description, then, can form a backdrop for the teaching we now find about how Christians should treat each other so as to guard the unity of the church. (Compare Ephesians 4:3.) We shall proceed, then, with this assumption: Paul the apostle, knowing that the church in Rome faced the danger of division, and sincere in his desire to visit them and get their help in his further mission work to the west, wrote to help them to see the importance of unity and to give them specific guidance in maintaining that unity.

As we make headway through the passage, we shall have to speculate some about what groupings Paul has in mind. We shall also look for clues to the concrete situation in which the Romans found themselves. But even more important, we shall find a number of general points of reference that can help us in similar situations. There is just one condition that Paul obviously took for granted, and that we must note in order to understand what he says here: open communication among Christians about substantive issues. If we are accustomed to dealing with disagreements or differences of opinion by not talking about them with one another, we cannot appreciate Paul's expectation of what these early Christians could accomplish. We must remember that they could not just transfer their church membership to another congregation or denomination when they disagreed with something in the church they were attending. There was but one church. It had no central meeting place, but rather met in small groups (some of these are named in chapter 16) in various homes and probably as a large congregation in borrowed facilities from time to time. Thus, if one wanted to remain a Christian and had a disagreement with another Christian, there was no option to working out the problem, unless one were ready to split the body. Let's see, then, how Paul proposes that Christians should deal with a potentially divisive situation.

The opening paragraph is similar to the others in the passage, including hints about the situation in Rome, ethical/theological principles, and guidance on how to apply the principles in the decision-making process in this specific case. The situation appears to have been a disagreement between people whose Christian faith permitted them to eat anything—meat (whether sacrificed to idols or not is not mentioned here), vegetables, and fruit—and people with scruples against eating certain things— probably specifically meat. Paul indicates that the vegetarians in this case are working from a position of weaker faith than that of the omnivores. But the important principle here is that the person is more important than his or her opinions or practices. The judgment of such opinions and practices is to be left to the Lord, who, Paul is sure, will make people stand independent of their opinions about such matters. Therefore, those who find themselves in such a disagreement should neither condemn nor disdain the persons on the other side of the issue. It is especially important that we note Paul's advice to both the strong and the weak. There is to be no tyranny of the weaker in the church. Neither condemnation nor disdain is appropriate. Nor is there any indication that Paul sees one as worse than the other.

Keeping in mind the importance of the person in the mind of the Lord, we can follow Paul's reasoning in the rest of the passage, where Paul adds what is either another element of the one disagreement or the basis of a second disagreement—the issue of holy days. It is not clear whether the reference is to Jewish festivals, pagan celebrations, or Christian special days. The importance once again is the disagreement and its potential for division.

From here on, Paul is careful not to identify himself with one side or the other. In fact, he does not even make clear whether the sides on the days issue are the same as those on the meat issue. The principle at work here is the individual's relationship to the Lord. A person can find various ways to glorify God. The important thing is that the person be fully convinced in his or her own mind. Paul will deal with this latter principle more fully later.

Verses 9-12 develop the Christian ethical principle on the basis of the salvation that Paul has so fully explicated in chapters 1—8. The basic Christian doctrines of salvation of all who believe through the death and resurrection of Christ and of the coming judgment of all by God should help us keep things in perspective. If we are all saved by the same person and event, then we are brothers, no matter how we may disagree with one another over details. If we must all take responsibility for our decisions before God, then we should be busy enough keeping ourselves straight, without condemning or disdaining a brother or sister. We note also that Paul does not hesitate to use the negative warning of the coming judgment to motivate his readers to treat others with respect. Although he customarily emphasizes the good news, he does not shrink from mentioning the darker possibilities.

So far Paul has been rather negative, emphasizing how we should not be relating to one another. Now he turns to more positive action: "Therefore let us stop passing judgment on one another" (Romans 14:13).

Paul practiced what he (and Jesus) preached by not being directly condemnatory himself. He does not make it clear that people are flaunting their freedom to eat meat, but he does state clearly that they should not do so (Romans 14:15, 16). The Christian has a positive responsibility for the other Christian's conscience. Admittedly, this is a hard thing to practice. It is difficult to decide to abstain from an activity that one sees as good so as not to cause a brother to stumble. Paul must have recognized this difficulty, since he imbedded in this paragraph one of his strongest motivational principles. He reminds us that when we are considering our fellow Christians, we are thinking about and ultimately acting toward persons who are so precious to God that His Christ was willing to die for them. Our egotism makes it easy to remember this in reference to ourselves and those with whom we agree; but our faith should remind us that it is true for every believer— and, in fact, for every human being. He then adds the reminder of the nature of the kingdom of God. Its primary elements are "righteousness, peace and joy" (Romans 14:17); and these are not produced by arguing and condemning, but by acting lovingly toward others. Such a life-style is possible only with the help of the Holy Spirit; but it is the only way we can truly serve Christ and be pleasing to God.

In verses 19-21, Paul extends his exhortation to positive action. He suggests a positive goal, cancels a possible negative result, and gives a very specific application. If "peace and mutual edification" (Romans 14:19) were the conscious aim of every congregational activity and relationship, our congregations would be truly attractive and influential. They would mirror the love and active mercy of Christ himself. As in the last paragraph, Paul reminds us again of a basic truth that should motivate us to act in the right way. When we look at the other person, no matter how different that person may seem, we should recognize in him or her the work of God. Every person is a creation of God; and every Christian is in the process of God's work of salvation. If we forget that, we do so to our own peril and to the peril of those with whom we come into contact. Surely we would not consciously do anything to cause the downfall of God's work of creation and redemption. Then we must not do anything to cause one of God's creatures and one of the objects of His work of redemption to stumble.

That is obviously important enough for us to sacrifice even one of our great freedoms in Christ. Recognizing the validity of eating anything, we should at the same time be willing to forego such eating for the sake of the brother or sister. As we see from Galatians and Acts, Paul is willing to fight for the Christian's right to eat whatever is available. But we see here and in 1 Corinthians and elsewhere that Paul recognizes a hierarchy of rights, freedoms, and responsibilities in the Christian life. As important as eating might be in some situations, it is secondary to the value of the individual and the unity of the church. As Christians, we must always balance our rights with our responsibilities, being ready to take the initiative to heal and maintain relationships within the church.

In verse 23, we find Paul's last mention of eating. Here he leaves behind the specific situation in Rome. But he is not yet finished with his ethical exhortations. Since he has pointed out that the specific issues are not as important as the person and the work of God, there is more to say. But here it is important to note the basic principles at work in the closing words of chapter 14. Our opinions are best kept between ourselves and God. It seems that too often the opposite is the case: we speak our opinions forcefully to one another and rarely utter them in prayer. Perhaps Paul knows from experience what happens when our opinions are opened to God in prayer. One finds it difficult to convince God that certain of our personal beliefs are important, whether or not they are true. It might help us to be more open with God about such things and be a bit more circumspect about them with our fellow Christians.

Finally, Paul states that the individual's own conviction or conscience or belief determines right and wrong in such cases where we have no clear word of prohibition from God. If I do something I am convinced I should not do, the result in me is the same guilt as would result from my breaking one of the Ten Commandments. Therefore, I should honor that in other people and not try to get them to do what they are not yet convinced they should do.

Now Paul leaves us with an exhortation that will apply to every one of us; and he does it while complimenting his readers. Chapter 15 opens with these four verses:

> We who are strong ought to bear with the failings of the weak and not to please ourselves. Each of us should please his neighbor for his good, to build him up. For even Christ did not please himself but, as it is written: "The insults of those who insult you have fallen on me." For everything that was written in the past was written to teach us, so that through endurance and the encouragement of the Scriptures we might have hope.

Only once has Paul in any way identified whom he meant by "the weak." In Romans 14:2, the vegetarian is characterized as the one "whose faith is weak." But most of us, whatever our opinions, would be loath to call ourselves weak. So the effect of Romans 15:1 is to give every reader the responsibility to tolerate those characteristics with which we disagree. The operative principle in this section is the imitation of Christ. After all, Christ is the only one who ever lived who had some right to please himself, and He refused to do so. His concern was for others, including us. It should not be too hard for us to have a similar attitude. We should be able at least to tolerate diversity in the church when we consider how much diversity Christ both tolerates and blesses. The quotation from Psalm 69:9 shifts us once again from the human sphere to the realization that the way we relate to one another is an aspect of our relationship with God. Jesus taught the same basic lesson with His picture of the last Judgment in Matthew 25:31-46, which climaxes in the sentence, "Whatever you did for one of the least of these . . . , you did for me" (Matthew 25:40). Paul then completes this section with a reminder of the authority of the Scriptures in the life of the Christian. They teach us; they encourage us; and they give us hope, if we read them while practicing the Christian life with endurance.

As is so often true, Paul at this point breaks into prayer. The brief intercession recorded in verses 5 and 6 is interesting both for its details and because of its position here. We should note that two of the elements connected with Scriptures in verse 4 are in this prayer connected to God. Bible study and prayer should never be separated, since in the first we hear God and in the second we speak to God. We are best able to be taught and encouraged by the Scriptures when we have opened ourselves to God in prayer. Paul now asks God to give the Romans the spirit of unity that he has been exhorting them to display and maintain. Following Jesus should cause us to walk more and more closely and in step with one another, until unity of heart allows us to be united in what we say. If such unity happens, God will be glorified.

The remainder of this passage brings the whole ethical exhortation to a climax, as Paul directs our thoughts again to the person of Christ and to what He has done for us. With a string of quotations taken from the three major divisions of the Hebrew Bible: the Law (Deuteronomy 32:43), the Prophets (Isaiah 11:10), and the Writings (Psalms 18:49 and 117:1), Paul shows that the whole range of the Scriptures of the Jews witnesses to the inclusion of the Gentiles in God's kingdom. Paul thus gives ultimate authority to his plea for unity in the church. As he shows in Ephesians 2:11-22, if God has broken down the barrier between Jews and Gentiles, there is no reason for disunity in His church. In addition to the Scriptures, Paul points out that Christ's ministry among the Jews had the purpose of including the Gentiles in the chorus of the glorification of God. For Paul, the former Pharisee, this must have been the biggest surprise in his faith in Christ. Once he had accepted the abolishment of the distinction between Jew and Gentile, it seems that he could not abide any other distinction in the kingdom.

So Paul's whole statement here begins with the exhortation to accept one another. The operative principle here is once again the example of Christ, but this time personalized. How has Christ accepted us? Unconditionally! "While we were still sinners" (Romans 5:8). The present verse could be seen not only as the climax of this whole passage, but as the aim of the whole epistle. The whole first eleven chapters focus on the unconditional nature of salvation by the grace of God. Sin had left humanity helpless and hopeless. Even the law had become part of the problem instead of a solution. That was the state of humanity when, by His coming and His sacrificial death and victorious resurrection, Christ showed that He accepted human beings. "Just as I am, without one plea, but that Thy blood was shed for me." This traditional hymn of decision reflects the situation accurately. And Paul says that's the way we are to accept one another. We have no right to demand a certain pattern of thinking or acting before we are willing to accept another person. Only by accepting one another without prerequisites can we reflect our Lord's love for humanity.

The result of such open acceptance will be praise to God, which should be the purpose of everything the Christian does. Is there a more keenly felt need among people today than acceptance? In a time when the divorce statistics are well publicized, when close family members live in different parts of the world, when extended families are a thing of the past in much of the world, and when trust of public officials is rare, people are acutely aware of the need of being accepted into a community. The early church was such a community because its members were aware of how they had been accepted into the family of God. The New Testament testifies in many places to the difficulty of living out such acceptance of one another; but difficulty did not cause those early Christians to despair or quit trying. The church in Rome, with its strong Jewish background and its large Gentile population, had good reasons to divide; but Paul did not want that to happen. The unity of the church is worth the effort. Good will among Christians is a vital part of God's plan of salvation. For this reason, Paul climaxed his letter to Rome with these exhortations to unity, basing them on the major facets of the Christian faith: the importance of the individual, the sovereignty of God, the lordship of Christ, the coming Judgment, the goodness of creation, the sacrificial death of Christ, the reality of the Holy Spirit, the importance of faith, the effectiveness of the Scriptures, and the example of the unconditional acceptance of Christ.

It is no surprise, then, that Paul concludes this passage with another prayer: "May the God of hope fill you with all joy and peace as you trust in him, so that you may overflow with hope by the power of the Holy Spirit" (Romans 15:13). Did the Roman Christians lack hope? Paul complimented them on their faith (Romans 1:8), but here he repeatedly prays for hope for them, as well as endurance and encouragement. We really cannot say for sure what their need was in this regard. We can say, however, that without hope that God's purpose will be accomplished—that Christ will ultimately be victorious—it is next to impossible to continue to work toward or maintain unity against all the barriers to unity that our sin is all too quick to erect. Again and again, the Christian is directed—even driven—to God, who by the power of the Holy Spirit gives hope, by which we can live with endurance the life He has made possible for us in Christ Jesus.

CHAPTER THIRTEEN

The Work of the Gospel and Its Results

Romans 15:14—16:27

There remains now for Paul only to draw the epistle to a conclusion with some personal statements. He first compliments his original readers (Romans 15:14) and explains again his motivation in writing to them (Romans 15:15, 16). He gives them again a glimpse of his personal ministry (Romans 15:17-22), and then he turns to his immediate plans (Romans 15:23-33). In chapter 16, he commends the woman who is bearing the letter for him and lists people whom he wishes to greet and people who send greetings to Rome. Three times in these verses he turns to prayer, this time to benedictions (Romans 15:33; 16:20, 25-27).

In Romans 1:8, Paul had congratulated the Roman Christians on their reputation for faith; here (Romans 15:14) he adds goodness, knowledge, and competence to teach. He has made it clear that he has no illusions about them; he knows that they are not perfect. But even when he tries to help them toward better living as Christians, he does not neglect opportunities to praise them for what they are already accomplishing. Brothers and sisters are like that. They praise and instruct one another, which, of course, makes accepting instruction much easier than it would be otherwise.

Such a sibling relationship in no way contradicts the divine commission to a priestly ministry to which Paul next turns. As in other epistles (especially Galatians), Paul notes once again that his gospel is not peculiar. He assumes that these believers in Rome, most of whom he has never met and none of whom (as far as we can tell) were converted by his preaching, hold the same understanding of the gospel of salvation and the life of the believer as he does. Thus, his message in this epistle will not be totally new to them, but will rather be a review—a reminder—of the gospel to which they had initially responded.

One aspect of Paul's understanding of his ministry that is frequently overlooked is his use of the term *grace*. We usually connect grace with salvation in Paul's system of thought, and one can hardly overestimate the role grace plays in that part of Paul's theology. However, this verse is not the only one where he connects grace with ministry. Galatians 1:15 shows that Paul had trouble separating his becoming a Christian from his call to ministry, both of which he connects with grace. Even clearer, in Ephesians 3:2-6, Paul refers to his specific ministry of proclaiming the gospel to the Gentiles as God's "grace." At the least, Paul sees every opportunity to serve the Lord as a great privilege. No chore is too lowly and no activity is too difficult for this evangelist who had been turned around by Christ; rather, he sees ministry as an unmerited gift of God to him.

Having spent so much time explaining in the epistle that all of God's mercy is offered now to both Jew and Gentile, Paul can now unequivocally identify his ministry as "to the Gentiles" (Romans 15:16). He understands the task of proclaiming the gospel as a "priestly" responsibility. He offers here just enough references for us to understand what he means by *priestly*. The priest was one commissioned to function between God and human beings. This was a two-way activity: bringing God's Word humanward and taking human response Heavenward. The Word of God is, as Paul has already made clear, the gospel of salvation. The offering from earth to Heaven is composed of the persons who offer themselves as living sacrifices (Romans 12:1). In Paul's case, these are primarily the Gentiles. As innocent as this verse might appear today, for Paul to call Gentiles "an offering acceptable to God, sanctified by the Holy Spirit" (Romans 15:16) indicates how far he has moved from his days as a Pharisee, when he would have had little or nothing to do with a Gentile. In the temple at Jerusalem, Gentiles were warned not to approach the Court of Israel at the risk of their lives. But in Christ, those same Gentiles are sanctified as an offering (not just the bringer of an offering) and judged acceptable to God.

It is no wonder that he would then say, "Therefore I glory in Christ Jesus in my service to God" (Romans 15:17). It might be helpful to note here the tendency by nearly everybody who studies Paul to assume that he was a very serious, even sour individual, who can hardly be imagined with a smile on his face. But if we read this verse and many others carefully, we must see a hint of joy—even enjoyment—in the man as he ministered. Certainly, he was serious about the task he had been given; but anybody who has preached the gospel knows what overflowing joy results in the soul of the preacher from a person's coming to faith by means of the preaching of the good news. Only another preacher can fully comprehend Paul's glorying in that service, which causes rejoicing in Heaven.

On the other hand, such glorying should never be in the abilities or successes of the preacher, but rather in the power of Christ (Romans 15:18, 19). Perhaps once again, only the preacher can fully appreciate the power of the Spirit in the preaching task. As often as the preacher is disappointed with the results of his finest efforts, the preacher is surprised by the results of some less laudable jobs. Did Paul also have those "off days" on which his sermons seemed to take on a life of their own and those "good days" when the sermons seemed to fall flat? We cannot know; but we can recognize that Paul never credited his command of rhetorical skills for the winning of souls. "I planted the seed, Apollos watered it, but God made it grow" (1 Corinthians 3:6) is not false modesty, even if Paul, as I believe, had good rhetorical skills. It is merely recognizing the reality of the power of the Spirit in the preaching of the Word, which has been called His sword (Ephesians 6:17).

Paul's next statement brings us back once again to see his strategy for this mission. He states clearly that his plan was both general (to preach where Christ was not known) and geographical (Jerusalem to Illyricum and then west). Paul was a pioneer. He saw his calling to open frontiers for the gospel and then leave the work of organizing and expanding to others. There is no indication here that this is the only mission style or that it is superior to others. In fact, the respect with which Paul treats Apollos, Timothy, Titus, and others indicates his vision of a great breadth of ministry. But he makes it clear here that he knew what his precise task was, and he set about it with a will and a plan. Now the first phase of that plan had been completed. Soon a second phase will open, a phase in which he would like to involve the Christians in Rome.

Paul's words in Romans 15:23-29 comprise a rather straightforward statement—a personal word in a personal letter—so it needs little comment. He is asking not just for friendship, and not just for room and board in Rome; he is requesting support for his mission to Spain. It appears that he wants to make Rome the headquarters for his work in the western part of the empire. Antioch, which had been his supporting and sending church heretofore, would be too distant to play this role at the western extent of the Mediterranean Sea. Rome would be ideal as a base of operations and source of supply. Whether or not Paul ever got to Spain is clouded in history. There are traditions that claim he did, but there is no compelling evidence. It is possible that he was released from his imprisonment in Rome long enough to make a trip to Spain; but it is also possible that he was kept under guard in Rome until his death (see Acts 28). Whichever happened, it is clear here that Paul had very well formulated plans for future service to his beloved Lord.

We also see just what he was preparing to do at the time of writing. The collection he had made among the churches in Greece had to be delivered to Jerusalem for the relief of the poor Christians there (see Acts 20:1-6 and 1 Corinthians 9). It is obvious that this act of kindness from one group of Christians to another was very important to Paul. Any such show of mercy is, of course, important; but the opportunity for the Gentile believers to help their Jewish sisters and brothers was even more important. They owed it to them, he pointed out; but it was also an opportunity to test the unity of the church. It was possible, Paul knew, for the Jews to reject both the gift and the people who brought it, whose names are recorded in Acts 20:4. So for several important reasons, the risk must be run.

This is the risk Paul has in mind as he continues with a request for prayers in his behalf (Romans 15:30-33). If the reader has not recently read Acts 21:17—23:35, this is the time to do it. There we are told of Paul's reception in Jerusalem. His service (both money and men) was well received by the saints there, but the unbelievers rioted, got him arrested, and plotted against his life. The apostle was obviously aware of the very real dangers awaiting him in Judea. The irony is that he eventually arrived in Rome (Acts 24—28) at the expense of the Roman government, but under guard to await trial before Caesar. In the last two verses of Acts, Luke describes that time in Rome in this way: "For two whole years Paul stayed there in his own rented house and welcomed all who came to see him. Boldly and without hindrance he preached the kingdom of God and taught about the Lord Jesus Christ." In the original Greek, the last word of the book is *unhindered*. That is as

Paul would have wished it; no matter what his personal circumstances, his desire was that the gospel should not be hindered.

Chapter 15 closes with another benediction. Whereas in verse 13 he referred to the God of hope, here in verse 33 it is the God of peace, as also in Romans 16:20. Hope and peace are, of course, important to people in times of trouble and threat. He shared those times with the saints in Rome, and he naturally wanted to share with them the blessing of the God who is the source of both hope and peace.

Personal Greetings (16:1-27)

Romans 16 is one of the most fascinating and puzzling chapters of the New Testament. It is full of names, a fact that has sparked controversies among scholars for centuries. The controversies arise because Paul claims (in Romans 1:10-13) that he is planning to visit these Christians for the very first time, and he indicates (in Romans 1:8) that his knowledge of the congregation comes from their reputation. The question naturally arises, then, of how he could be acquainted with so many individuals, families, and groups of Christians in Rome. Many scholars have speculated that this chapter originally closed a letter to Ephesus, where he had spent much time and developed many relationships. However, even though there are many problems with the Greek text of this chapter, there is no good evidence that the whole chapter was ever attached to anything other than the epistle to Rome.

We may without great difficulty assume that the chapter belongs right where it appears. We tend to forget how much travel was possible for citizens of the Roman Empire. We forget also the relative ease of communication. Compared to what is available in our modern era, of course, first-century travel and correspondence were primitive; but they were possible for most people, especially for Roman citizens and residents of the capital. We know from Acts 18 that Paul had not only met, but also worked with, Aquila and Priscilla. They had left Rome earlier because of an edict of Emperor Claudius and traveled to Corinth, where they established a business. They are the first two residents of Rome whom Paul greets in this chapter, and we can assume that the others mentioned also met Paul somewhere on his journeying or else were part of that reputation of which he wrote in chapter 1.

More important than such controversy and speculation is the glimpse we get in this chapter of the reality of the church in Rome and of the importance of Christian relationships transcending geographical limitations. In chapters 12—15, we saw both theoretical and practical references to the reality of the church. But here, we are in touch with actual people, some living in Italy, some in Greece, and at least two traveling. Let's look at these people to see something of the first-century church.

The first person mentioned is a woman named Phoebe, "a servant of the church in Cenchrea" (Romans 16:1). This is the only place in the New Testament where we find the name *Phoebe;* but the few words said about her reveal a lot. The position of this statement, at the head of the list of greetings, indicates that Phoebe was carrying the letter for Paul to Rome. Was she a businesswoman in Cenchrea on a trip to Rome? Was she visiting relatives there? We don't know whether there was a reason for her visit other than to carry Paul's letter, but it is not too speculative to assume that there was.

Phoebe's position in the church at Cenchrea appears to have been important. The word translated "servant" is a form of the word *diakonos,*[30] from which, of course, we get our word *deacon.* It is hard to be sure in many places where this word appears whether or not it denotes some sort of official office in the church. In fact, we have a strong tendency to assume some sort of American/democratic structure any time we read a term like this. If Paul meant that Phoebe had been elected to some responsibility, he leaves us in the dark about it. What is clear is that she was a respected worker in the congregation in her city, which was the seaport of Corinth. She most likely was a person of substance, since she was able to be of help to many people, including a traveler like Paul, with his retinue of companions.

Phoebe obviously needed some help in Rome—a place to stay, an introduction to the city or to specific people, or help to get to yet another destination. Equally obviously, Paul felt free to request such help from the believers in the capital. Such open hospitality appears to have been a characteristic of the earliest church. People who had been redeemed by the grace of Christ could no longer be selfish with themselves, their time, or their possessions. They considered whatever they had to belong to the Heavenly Father, and thus to all of His children. So Phoebe could travel

---

[30]Surprisingly enough, this word is *diakonon,* a masculine form.

from Cenchrea to Rome with the expectation that this letter from Paul would cause her to be welcomed into the fellowship of sisters and brothers in the capital.

The first Romans named by Paul in the list of greetings that follows are his old friends from Corinth. It is possible that they also were acquainted with Phoebe, from their time in Corinth, but there is no indication of that here. The first time this couple appears on the pages of the book of Acts (18:1), the man is named first, but the three times they are named later in that chapter, the names appear in the same order as in this list of Paul's: "Priscilla and Aquila" (Romans 16:3). It is interesting to speculate about why the wife would be mentioned before her husband, but again that would be just speculation. What we can be assured of is that their Christian service (and perhaps also their business) was performed as a team. It is possible that Paul directed Phoebe to their house first, so that they would then see to it that his letter was made known to the rest of the church in Rome. At any rate, he commends their life-risking service to him and, as a result, to the whole of the church among the Gentiles. He is probably referring here to something that happened in Corinth, perhaps to a detail of the risk the Christians there had faced because of an uproar in the court of Gallio, the Proconsul (Acts 18). Such mutual experience makes persons conscious of being fellow workers, dependent on and responsible for one another.

"Greet also the church which meets at their house" (Romans 16:5). It appears that this couple was no less active in Rome than they had been in Corinth. Their home was one of the meeting places of the church at Rome. As we shall see, Paul mentions in verse 15 another such group. It is most likely that since the church had not yet developed buildings specifically dedicated for meetings for worship or teaching, they met regularly in relatively small groups with the families who had homes large enough to accommodate them. Some Roman homes could easily hold meetings of fifty people in an open area surrounded by porches. The whole church in a city would then likely arrange meetings in a large facility (or out of doors) when a reason arose. The arrival of a letter from Paul the apostle would likely be such an occasion, so that everybody could hear read the words of the famous missionary.

Next, Paul greets Epenetus, a man whom he had first met in Asia, perhaps in Ephesus (Acts 19) or perhaps earlier in a village in the interior of what we now call Asia Minor. Paul neither takes credit for this man's conversion nor locates that conversion on the map. He merely greets him in Rome. Thus we begin to see the global nature of the church in Rome.

Next he mentions the third woman on the list: "Greet Mary, who worked very hard for you" (Romans 16:6). *Miriam* is a common Hebrew name, and this could be its Roman form, but it could also be the feminine form of the Roman name *Marius;* so we can't even tell if this woman is Jewish or Gentile. Of course, this fact was not important to Paul, since one of his main points in the letter was the abolishing of the distinction between Jew and Gentile. Where Mary worked for them is also not stated. She might have done something significant with Paul somewhere to help establish the validity of Gentile Christianity. Or he might have heard of her labors as part of the church's reputation.

Verse 7 presents us with another interesting question, along with some insight into the history of the transmission of the text of the New Testament. The second name listed here is usually translated "Junias," but the decision about whether it is a man's name or a woman's ("Junia") depends in the Greek on the placement of the accent mark. The fact that the masculine form of this name has not been found anywhere else in all of literature is strong evidence that Paul is here referring to a woman, probably the wife of Andronicus. The further fact that later accented texts and many (although far from all) commentators have read the name as masculine probably indicates more about the male expectation that Paul would not refer to a woman in the terms he uses in this verse than about the facts in the case.

Paul makes four statements about this couple. First, he says that they are his relatives. It is unclear how close this relationship might be. It could merely refer to them as fellow Jews; but since Paul says three more things about them, it is likely that the relationship was familial and that they had known Paul in the East— that is, in Tarsus, Jerusalem, or Antioch. Second, he says that they were fellow prisoners. Again it is not clear that he means (as the NIV states it) that the three of them were in the same prison at the same time, although that is possible. What is important to Paul is that they had this experience in common. Third, he describes them in terms that have caused many to decide that he was referring to two men: "outstanding among the apostles." The original Greek is just as ambiguous here as is the English. Was he calling them apostles and commending them as outstanding ones, or did he mean that the apostles considered them as outstanding Christians? Although the term *apostle* is used in a very general way (meaning missionary) at times in the New Testament, it is more likely that here Paul means simply that even the apostles respected this couple. And fourth, Paul admits once again (see 1 Corinthians 15:8) that he was a relative latecomer into Christ. One would like to know what role these people might have played in Paul's early development as a Christian, but we have no information about them except these tantalizing hints. We can only share Paul's respect for Andronicus and Junia as experienced Christians whose commitment had placed them in prison at least once and whose service had gained them a fine reputation among the apostles. How many such unsung heroes must there have been to guide and motivate the church in its tremendous growth in those early years?

About Ampliatus we know nothing except Paul's affection for him (Romans 16:8). We are equally unfamiliar with Urbanus and Stachys (Romans 16:9). We are once again frustrated, but amazed, at how many of these Roman Christians Paul was acquainted with. One wonders, however, what it might have meant to be named as beloved or friend or fellow-worker of the apostle to the Gentiles.

Apelles is said to have been "tested and approved in Christ" (Romans 16:10). This designation is a translation of one Greek word—the same one Paul has used in Romans 12:2 in reference to the Christian's transformation resulting in the "testing and approving" of what the will of God is. It is like a seal of approval on both the life of the individual and the will of God.

In the last half of verse 10 and in verse 11, we have three names, but reference to unnamed and unnumbered others. It could be that both Aristobulus and Narcissus were heads of large households, which would likely include slaves along with family members. It is also possible that their personal households formed the nucleus of what are commonly called house churches. And between those references stands Herodian, another kinsman of Paul. Jews and Gentiles continue to be listed without distinction.

Tryphena and Tryphosa (Romans 16:12) must have been sisters, if not twins, judging from their names. Who wouldn't like to know more about them? And with his greeting to Persis, it appears that Paul is running short of ways to compliment people.

For the first time he repeats with only a slight change his description: they "work hard in the Lord."

"Greet Rufus, chosen in the Lord, and his mother, who has been a mother to me, too" (Romans 16:13). We can't be sure what Paul had in mind with the word *chosen* here, since he used this term to refer to all Christians, but we do find the name Rufus in Mark 15:21, referring to one of the sons of Simon of Cyrene, who carried the cross of our Lord for a time. We are also reminded once again of the deep respect that Paul had for women in the church and the service they performed for fellow believers; but if Rufus's mother had been married to that Simon, her memories would be especially precious.

Verses 14 and 15 complete this list by mentioning nine more people by name and a number of others. One can't read very much out of these names. Some have suggested that they could all be either slaves or former slaves, but we can't be sure. What we do notice, once again, is reference to groups of Christians connected with them. It could be that those named are the family members in whose houses the groups (brothers and saints) met.

It seems amazing that there are still people who claim that Paul was prejudiced against women. Of the twenty-eight persons individually named in this chapter so far, ten of them are women, most of whom get the same kind of praise as do the men. Here is good evidence for the reality of what the apostle spells out in theory in Galatians 3:28: "There is neither Jew nor Greek, slave nor free, male nor female, for you are all one in Christ Jesus."

The actual greeting is concisely stated in verse 16: "Greet one another with a holy kiss. All the churches of Christ send greetings." However the kiss was practiced, it appears to have been a widespread custom among Christians. It is mentioned in 1 Corinthians 16:20; 2 Corinthians 13:12; and 1 Thessalonians 5:26. Justin Martyr a century later mentioned it as a regular part of the worship practice in Rome. The practice certainly demonstrated the close (familial) relationship that characterized the fellowship of the early church. Paul is probably not exaggerating when he greets them from all the churches, since this close fellowship obviously transcended geographical, political, and racial boundaries. He has already pointed to their reputation, which he had encountered in his travels; he can, therefore, with some confidence, offer them greetings from everybody. Such open relationships among Christians appears often enough in the church today that we can appreciate Paul's freedom to communicate in this personal way. Such fellowship is so important that all Christians ought to work hard to develop and maintain it.

In verses 17-19, Paul inserts yet another bit of teaching, this time in the form of a warning against "those who cause divisions and put obstacles in your way that are contrary to the teaching you have learned" (Romans 16:17). As Paul makes clear in Galatians 1:6-9 and other places, there was recognized in the church even as early as twenty years after the death and resurrection of Jesus a body of doctrine (teaching) that was trustworthy. It is also clear that some people were teaching things that were not part of the pure gospel. In 1 Corinthians 15, and in more detail here in Romans, Paul outlines the essential gospel. His custom appears to have been to emphasize the positive, that is, the truth. But he was also moved at times to warn his readers in no uncertain terms against the false teachers. He is careful not to help these enemies of the faith by discussing in detail their teachings, but rather he urges people to compare all teachings with what they have learned and what is accepted by all the churches.

His final advice here is helpful for all Christians. The Lord is best served when we major in the study of the good and keep ourselves some distance from the evil. We should notice one more thing here: obedience is the key. For the Christian, orthodoxy is never enough. Correct thinking stops short of what is demanded of the follower of Christ unless it leads to appropriate living. In Romans 1:8, he mentioned that the faith of the Roman believers was well known; now he refers to their obedience. The two are never separable in the mind and experience of Paul.

Verse 20 is Paul's last promise and benediction: "The God of peace will soon crush Satan under your feet. The grace of our Lord Jesus be with you." The expectation that stems from Genesis 3, that God's ultimate dealing with sin will mean the bruising or crushing of the serpent's head, is a refrain that must have been recognizable in Paul's teaching and preaching on a regular basis. But here he involves Christians themselves in the fulfillment of the prophecy. *Under your feet* invites every disciple of Jesus into the cosmic struggle between God and Satan for the destiny of humankind. Only by the grace of Jesus dare we hope to succeed. But Paul phrases this most awesome challenge in the form of promise and benediction. There is no doubt about the outcome because the power to accomplish it is "the grace of our Lord Jesus."

The next three verses list eight people who are with Paul and who wish to send greetings to Rome: Timothy, Lucius, Jason, Sosipater, Tertius, Gaius, Erastus, and Quartus. Timothy we know about from Acts 16 and other references, especially the two epistles that bear his name as recipient. The name Lucius appears in Acts 13:1 as a leader of the church in Antioch, a man of Cyrene. A Jason is mentioned in Acts 17:5-9, who made his house in Thessalonica available for Paul and got into trouble over it. Sosipater's name is not found elsewhere in the New Testament, although one very similar (Sopater) appears in Acts 20:4, in the list of men accompanying Paul on the journey during which he wrote this letter. We can't be sure of the identities of these men, but a look at the possibilities reminds us again of the universal nature of the church.

The very simple personal greeting in verse 22 gives us another glimpse of Paul's methods. It is obvious that Paul used, as was the custom of most letter writers of his day, a scribe or stenographer (amanuensis) to take down his dictated epistles. Here we have the only place where this person is named. In fact, he is permitted to write this verse himself, designating himself (with some pleasure, I think) as the writer. Tertius is not well known, but consider how important he and others like him have been in the transmission of the written Word of God. It is not only famous people who are important. In fact, there is evidence (see Galatians 6:11 and consider the possibility that Paul's eyesight or some physical problem would not allow him to write well) that without such help we would have very little, if anything, from Paul's mind.

Gaius is obviously the head of a household in whose home the whole church in Corinth could gather. His name appears also in Acts 20:4 and 1 Corinthians 1:14, as one of the few in Corinth who were baptized personally by Paul.

Erastus has been the focus of much study and speculation over the years. His name appears in Acts 19:22 as one of Paul's helpers who, along with Timothy, was sent ahead into Macedonia earlier on this same journey and in 2 Timothy 4:20, where Paul says that he stayed in Corinth. His designation here as "director of public works" may or may not indicate that there are two men with the same name on this trip. At any rate, Erastus appears to have been an important city official in Corinth at the time. A marble block has been unearthed as part of a street in first-century Corinth bearing the name Erastus, director of public works. The Greek designation in Romans 16:23 is that of the city treasurer, but it is possible that the same person bore both titles. It is apparent that by this time not all Christians in Corinth were poor peasants and slaves.

About Quartus we know nothing except what Paul states here.

As is Paul's custom, he ends the letter with a doxology. He sometimes uses a benediction, but he has already done that in verse 20. This doxology is not only an ascription of praise to God, but it also neatly summarizes the content of the whole epistle.

> Now to him who is able to establish you by my gospel and the proclamation of Jesus Christ, according to the revelation of the mystery hidden for long ages past, but now revealed and made known through the prophetic writings by the command of the eternal God, so that all nations might believe and obey him—to the only wise God be glory forever through Jesus Christ! Amen.

It appears that what Paul has intended all along with this epistle is to establish the Christians in Rome. He has carefully developed his understanding of the gospel, beginning with the human predicament in sin, dealing with the results of Christ's sacrificial death and resurrection and how a person can obtain those by means of obedient faith, continuing to deal with specific questions about God's strategy (mystery) of Jew-Gentile relationships, and looking toward the future when all of God's creation will be redeemed. He has then related all of that to the way Christians are to live in the community of faith and in their societies. All of this was apparently involved in his proclamation of Jesus the Christ, a task that he hopes to perform in Rome.

Furthermore, Paul sees all of this gospel and proclamation as part of God's revelation of His plan for the redemption of the world, a plan that only now has become clear, but has been there to be discovered in the writings of the prophets. The focus of that plan, as Paul proclaims it, is the gospel's result "that all nations might believe and obey him." Paul's writings, as well as Luke's portrayal of Paul in Acts, are consistent in this—that God is now opening His kingdom to the Gentile as well as to the Jew. Paul's gospel has been from the beginning of his ministry a message to all nations, an emphasis that is in perfect harmony with Christ's commission to His disciples, as recorded in the Gospels.

Even in Paul's day, the nations were not neatly divided by geographic or political borders. Those nations *(ethne)* were then, as they are now, mixed together in the cities of the world; and Paul seems to have fully expected the church in each city to display the results of the gospel as did the churches in Antioch and Rome, where Jews and Gentiles, people of various races and nationalities, were united in their common faith in Jesus Christ. Nobody knew better than Paul the problems that accompany such a mix. But nobody appreciated more than he did the importance in an age of division and alienation of a fellowship in which people could find reconciliation and unity. It is no wonder that for the early church, evangelism and unity were equally important concerns. One who is truly (in faith and obedience) converted to Christ will naturally seek unity with others of like precious faith. A congregation that displays that sort of unity will naturally be attractive to persons who yearn for real reconciliation.

Of course, Paul's ultimate concern is not success, as that is judged by humans, but glory to God. This God, who has revealed himself and His plan of salvation through His Son, Jesus Christ, will be glorified best by people who involve themselves totally in the stream of redemption, whose source is the very heart of God. Such involvement demands the sacrifice of self, which Paul has pictured in chapter 12. It involves taking the initiative in developing and maintaining personal relationships, as he has described in chapters 14 and 15. It promises risks in ministry, which Paul recognizes in Romans 15:30-32. But it also pledges the unending love and ultimate glory that Paul outlines in chapter 8. To enjoy the love that reached out to us when we were helpless, made us new creations, will not let us go, and promises us glory for eternity is worth whatever it takes to get it. It takes the "obedience of faith," a life of loyalty shown in living the only life appropriate for such redeemed ones—the life of God's love, which He pours into our hearts for us to give to others. Such a life will give glory to God forever, through Jesus Christ. Amen.

SUGGESTED READING

Augustinus, Aurelius. *The Confessions of Saint Augustine.* Trans. Edward B. Pusey. New York: Pocket Books, 1957.

Bainton, Roland. *Here I Stand.* New York: The American Library of World Literature, 1950.

Barrett, C. K. *A Commentary on the Epistle to the Romans.* London: Adam & Charles Black, 1973.

Barth, Karl. *The Epistle to the Romans.* Trans. Edwyn C. Hoskyns. Oxford: Oxford University Press, 1975.

Bornkamm, Gunther. *Geschichte und Glaube II.* Munich: Chr. Kaiser Verlag, 1971.

Charlesworth, James H., ed. *The Old Testament Pseudepigrapha.* Garden City, NY: Doubleday, 1983.

Cicero. *De Re Publica and De Legibus* (Loeb Classic Library, *Cicero,* Vol. 16). Cambridge, Massachusetts: Harvard University Press, 1970.

Cranfield, C. E. B. *A Critical and Exegetical Commentary on the Epistle to the Romans.* Edinburgh: T. & T. Clark, 1975.

Cranfield, C. E. B. *Romans: A Shorter Commentary.* Grand Rapids: William B. Eerdmans, 1985.

Davies, W. D. *Paul and Rabbinic Judaism: Some Rabbinic Elements in Pauline Theology.* Philadelphia: Fortress Press, 1980.

Dillenberger, John. *Martin Luther.* Garden City, NY: Doubleday, 1961.

Donfried, Karl P., ed. *The Romans Debate*. Minneapolis: Augsburg, 1977.

Justin Martyr. "Apology I," in *Writings of Saint Justin Martyr*. Thomas B. Falls, ed. (in the series, *The Fathers of the Church*) New York: Christian Heritage, Inc., 1948.

Luther, Martin. *Lectures on Romans*. Wilhelm Pauck, ed. Philadelphia: Westminster, 1961.

William Sanday and Arthur C. Headlam. *A Critical and Exegetical Commentary on the Epistle to the Romans*. Edinburgh: T. & T. Clark, 1977.

Sanders, E. P. *Paul and Palestinian Judaism*. Philadelphia: Fortress Press, 1977.

Sweeney, Z. T. *New Testament Christianity*. Columbus, IN: published privately, 1923.

Tennyson, Alfred. *Idylls of the King*.

Wesley, John. *The Journal of John Wesley*. Percy L. Parker, ed. Chicago: Moody Press, n. d.

Wilckens, Ulrich. *Der Brief an die Roemer*. Zurich: Benziger Verlag, 1978, 1980, 1982.